THE FUTURE OF THE INTERNATIONAL MONETARY SYSTEM

Publications of the John F.Kennedy Institute
Center for International Studies, Tilburg, the Netherlands
Nr. 4

Published in cooperation with the Société Universitaire Européenne de
Recherches Financières (SUERF)

THE FUTURE OF THE INTERNATIONAL MONETARY SYSTEM

edited by
HANS W. J. BOSMAN
and
FRANS A. M. ALTING VON GEUSAU

with contributions by

PAUL BAREAU
EDWARD M. BERNSTEIN
IRVING S. FRIEDMAN
MILTON GILBERT
EMILE VAN LENNEP

JAVIER MÁRQUEZ
J. PETRIVALSKÝ
ROBERT W. RUSSELL
L. VELTRUSKÝ

A. W. SIJTHOFF—LEYDEN

1970

Heath Lexington Books
D. C. Heath and Company
Lexington, Massachusetts

ISBN 90 218 9120 4 Sijthoff

Library of Congress Catalog Card Number: 78-124498
© A. W. Sijthoff's Uitgeversmaatschappij, N.V. 1970

Printed in the Netherlands by A. W. Sijthoff, Printing Division, Leyden

Published in the United States of America by Heath LEXINGTON Books,
D. C. Heath and Company, Lexington, Massachusetts

PREFACE

The problems of the post-war international monetary system and its frequent crises, especially in recent years, have led to many publications and conferences dealing with the causes of this instability and the possibility of improving the system. So far most discussions have taken place between monetary experts and have been restricted to proposals for various schemes for improving international liquidity.

They have also been restricted to the problems of convertible currencies and the activities of IMF and the Group of Ten. The future of the international monetary system, however, is as much an international and political problem as a monetary matter. It requires that policy-makers and monetary experts alike pay increasing attention not only to the problems of convertible currencies but also to the role of the socialist countries in reshaping the monetary system and to the problems which face the developing countries in fostering economic development.

To meet this need for a broader discussion between policy-makers and experts, the Société Universitaire Européenne de Recherches Financières and the John F. Kennedy Institute jointly organized a colloquium on The Future of the International Monetary System, which was held at Tilburg in the Netherlands, from April 16-19, 1969.

The SUERF was established in 1964 with the object of promoting and conducting research into financial problems on a European basis. For this purpose it seeks to attract individuals from academic and research institutions, banking and the world of finance, and members of national and international administrations.

The John F. Kennedy Institute, center for international studies, was established in 1966. As an interdisciplinary research center its objective is to contribute to the study of relations between countries in the Atlantic area and the place and significance of these countries in promoting peaceful international relations. SUERF was happy to be able to draw on the experience the Kennedy Institute had gained in organizing colloquia in recent years.

The Kennedy Institute, for its part, could draw on the SUERF Steering Committee's knowledge of monetary problems and of those able to discuss them.

We felt that such a presentation by able scholars would be necessary if we were to have a thorough discussion of these problems at the colloquium.

We also felt that discussions in this field are more frequent in the USA than in Europe, which was another reason we took the initiative in organising this meeting, to which monetary specialists, bankers, political scientists and politicians were invited.

The present book contains, in Chapters II-VII, revised texts of the papers prepared for the colloquium. Chapter I is the revised text of the opening address by Mr. E. van Lennep. Chapter VIII contains a summary of the major issues dealt with in the preceding chapters and during discussions at the colloquium: it was drafted by Mr. Paul Bareau when the discussions were over and rewritten afterwards for inclusion in this volume. It should be borne in mind that all the chapters were written before April 1969. Although they were revised later, none of the authors has been asked to include developments which have occurred since.

Chapter II, by Mr. Milton Gilbert, deals with the general problem of the present imbalances in international payments caused by the current account position of several countries as well as by abnormally large capital movements. The situation in different parts of the world is thoroughly analysed. The author also deals with the disequilibrium which, in his opinion, exists in the monetary system as such.

What is already being done in the field of multilateral surveillance and the adjustment process is analyzed in Chapter III by Mr. Robert W. Russell. Although it seems that multilateral surveillance, as practised especially in Working Party no. 3 of the Economic Policy Committee of the OECD, has little influence on policy decisions, the author thinks that these activities can be considered valuable because of the possibilities offered to participants to learn about the background of each other's policies.

Foremost in the discussion on international monetary issues stands the future of international reserve assets, which is the subject of Chapter IV, written by Mr. Edward M. Bernstein. He underlines the idea that the growth of aggregate reserve assets should be sufficient to provide countries with the means of financing deficits without relying on deflation or on trade and exchange restrictions. He welcomes the creation of the Special Drawing Rights Scheme which took effect at the annual meeting of the IMF in September 1969. In order, however, to maintain the equivalence of all reserve assets in international settlements, Mr. Bernstein elaborates on the idea of establishing a Reserve Settlement Account.

After these more general aspects, specific questions are raised in the following chapters.

Mr. Javier Márquez discusses in Chapter V the role of the developing countries in the international monetary system. He takes a critical view of the SDR scheme, as it fails to take into account the special needs of the developing countries.

Mr. Irving S. Friedman deals in Chapter VI with the implications of structural problems in the international monetary management of development finance. Emphasizing the real phenomena underlying monetary data, he considers some of the ways in which the prevailing types of balance of payments analysis fail to embrace broad structural, political and social considerations.

In Chapter VII, Professors Veltruský and Petrivalský point out how the prevailing situation and regulations in and between the Comecon countries influence the relation of this part of the world to the international monetary system. They indicate in what direction this relation might change in the future.

We hope that by bringing together these studies by eminent scholars, we shall illuminate certain new aspects of this important problem.

The editors are indebted to the "Economisch Instituut Tilburg", the "Netherlands Instituut voor het Bank- en Effectenbedrijf" and several banks in Western Europe for sponsoring the colloquium, and to Sijthoff publishers for publishing the present volume. They are particularly grateful to Mr. R. J. Hollingdale for correcting and revising the manuscripts. They would also like to express their sincere gratitude to the members of their respective staffs for their willingness to assist in preparing the colloquium and to Mr. J. Koning and Mr. F. Engering for assisting in preparing the publication of this volume.

Without the invaluable and unwearied assistance of Miss M. C. Hinkenkemper, secretary to the colloquium and to the two cooperating organizations, and Miss A. Vugs, assistant to the secretary, this volume could not have been published.

F. A. M. Alting von Geusau
H. W. J. Bosman

ABOUT THE AUTHORS

Frans A. M. Alting von Geusau (editor) is professor of the Law of International Organizations at Tilburg University and Director of the John F. Kennedy Institute. He is the author of "European Organizations and Foreign Relations of States. A Comparative Analysis of Decision-Making" and of "Beyond the European Community" as well as of several studies on European Integration, the United Nations and problems of peace and world order.

Hans W. J. Bosman (editor) is professor of Money, Credit and Banking at Tilburg University and Chairman of the "Société Universitaire Européenne de Recherches Financières (SUERF). He is the author of books on the law of credit control in the Netherlands and on international monetary aspects and wrote several studies on Dutch banking and national and international monetary problems.

Emile van Lennep was at the time of the Colloquium Treasurer General of the Netherlands, Chairman of the Monetary Committee of the European Economic Community (EEC) and Chairman of Working Party 3 of the Organization for Economic Cooperation and Development (OECD). Mr. van Lennep is Secretary General of OECD since October 1, 1969.

Milton Gilbert is Economic Adviser and Head of the Monetary and Economic Department, Bank for International Settlements (BIS).

Robert W. Russell was Assistant Professor of Political Science, Wisconsin State University. From September 1, 1970, Northern Illinois University, U.S.A.

Edward Bernstein has been Director, Research and Statistics Department of the International Monetary Fund. At the moment he is a member of E.M.B. Ltd, Washington.

Javier Márquez is Director, Centro de Estudios Monetarios Latin-americanos, Mexico.

Irving S. Friedman is Economic Adviser, International Bank for Reconstruction and Development (Worldbank) Washington.

Ladislav Veltruský and Jiri Petrivalský are Rector respectively Professor, High School of Economics, Prague.

Paul Bareau is Economic Adviser to the International Press Company (IPC).

TABLE OF CONTENTS

LIST OF TABLES

ABBREVIATIONS USED

BIS	Bank for International Settlements
CIAP	Comite Internacional Alianza Progreso
COMECON	Council for Mutual Economic Assistance
CRU	Collective Reserve Unit
DM	German Mark
EEC	European Economic Community
ECOSOC	Economic and Social Council
f.o.b.	Free on board
GAB	General Arrangements to Borrow
GATT	General Agreement on Tariffs and Trade
GNP	Gross National Product
IBRD	International Bank for Reconstruction and Development
IMF	International Monetary Fund
LDC(s)	Less Developed Countrie(s)
NATO	North Atlantic Treaty Organization
OECD	Organization for Economic Cooperation and Development
SDR(s)	Special Drawing Right(s)
UK	United Kingdom
UNCTAD	United Nations Conference on Trade and Development
US	United States

Chapter I

INTRODUCTION

by *Emile van Lennep*

The subjects discussed in this book, cover a very wide field. It is certainly an appropriate time for a comparison of the views experts have reached on these urgent problems as the result of careful study. There are large payments imbalances which nations are seeking to correct. There is a widespread feeling that the present international monetary system has somehow become inherently unstable. Both problems have led to a number of proposals whereby the present monetary system would be modified or replaced. Moreover, the ratification and possible implementation of the Special Drawing Rights Scheme in the IMF are of present interest.

Two main views on the causes of the present problems can be distinguished in the following chapters. One view is that the problems are mainly the reflection of inadequate adjustment policies on the part of the countries where disequilibria are most apparent—and an inadequate international co-ordination of individual policies. On this view, the solutions lie primarily in steps to be taken *within* the framework of the existing monetary system, though some modifications to the system would be helpful. The second view is that it is the internal monetary system itself which is mainly at fault. While holders of this view would not, generally, disagree that there is scope for better individual adjustment policies, they maintain that these cannot bear their full fruit unless the system itself is fairly radically changed.

The present payments imbalances are described in chapter II by Mr. Gilbert. The main features of the picture are clear. The United States current account is far too weak, despite the countercyclical measures which, progressively, the authorities have been taking to combat the overheating of the economy. The United Kingdom's balance of payments, in 1968 as a whole, showed disappointing progress after the decision to devalue and the subsequent series of domestic measures. In France the social disturbances of last summer have led to the emergence of a current account deficit and substantial intermittent capital flight reflecting confidence factors. Germany and Italy, on the other hand, have been running massive surpluses on current account which look like persisting for some time to come. Both these creditor countries have to offset these surpluses by equally massive capital outflows; in the case of Germany, these capital exports rely partly on monetary policy attitudes which may become more difficult to maintain in an atmosphere of rising demand pressures; and in the case of Italy, massive capital exports accord ill with domestic needs. Looking at the position as a whole, the striking point is not just the size of some of the deficits and surpluses, but the large and persistent difference between the balance of payments results of the major countries and the external targets they aim at.

The first thing we have to ask ourselves is how far we could reasonably hope that, with better economic policies, we could overcome the present payments imbalances and avoid their repetition on the present scale and for their present duration. It is not difficult for the observer to put his finger on faults of omission or commission in the demand management policies of both debtors and creditors in recent years. There have been cases of inadequate action on the part of governments resulting from political difficulties (not all governments, after the event, would think that they had gained politically from such decisions); and there have been cases where action has been inadequate for more technical reasons—because the situation was not assessed properly by the experts, or because the most appropriate policy weapons were not available. I would think that no one would deny that we can reasonably expect countries to aim at better adjustment policies.

But how far can we reasonably expect progress in this direction to go? The very fact that payments imbalances of countries with relatively sophisticated administrative machines and electorates have remained so large for so long must make us wonder whether we have been trying to tackle the imbalances in the wrong way. Obviously, a certain degree of inefficiency in correcting imbalances has to be tolerated, because political circumstances are what they are and because governmental omniscience is not to be expected. But a better internationl harmonization of national economic aims and priorities would be needed, and a more complete and balanced use of the policy mix of budget, monetary and incomes policies could be achieved. Can we expect these policies for correcting imbalances to be substantially better than in recent years? If not, we might have to add to our present adjustment policy efforts certain other elements.

One possible new element is suggested in a paper which Mr. Houthakker prepared before he joined the Council of Economic Advisers.[1] It may, according to Mr. Houthakker, be necessary to achieve a better external equilibrium in a more direct way, namely by moving away from the present system of a fixed (though variable) exchange rate to "the self-adjusting peg" with the bands somewhat wider than the 1 per cent current today.

Another view of the causes of the present payments imbalances is put forward by Mr. Gilbert at the end of Chapter II. Mr. Gilbert, in effect, suggests that we are hitting our heads against a brick wall. Very briefly, his argument is that there is a shortage of "ultimate reserves" which renders it virtually impossible for deficit countries—whatever their efforts may be—to correct their positions of imbalance. Most countries feel they need to see their official reserves rise and prefer this rise to take the form of additional gold holdings. Given the shortage of new gold, this is difficult. Under these conditions the world as a whole can increase its gross reserves only at the cost of an increase of liabilities on the part of the countries whose currencies are considered "international"—in other words, the desired increase of total gross reserves can be achieved only so long as some countries have substantial official settlements deficits. This line of thought of Mr. Gilbert leads easily on to discussion of the problem of international reserve creation.

---

1. H. Houthakker: "De toekomst van het internationale monetaire bestel", *Economisch Kwartaaloverzicht Amsterdam-Rotterdam Bank N.V.*, nr. 15, december 1968.

It is here that we come up against the second main problem referred to in this book. What are the reasons for suspecting that there is now an *instability of the system*? There are obvious reasons. When the United States and the United Kingdom run deficits of so large a size for so long a time, confidence in the future purchasing power of the dollar and the pound sterling must obviously weaken. For many years now the position has been reached—and probably accepted as a continuing state of affairs —that liabilities in sterling have gone about as far as they can go. Apart from official swap holdings, UK liabilities have changed in country-distribution but not substantially in total for a number of years. US liabilities, on the other hand, have frequently increased substantially, and this has at least till recently led to a fairly widespread feeling that dollars were too plentiful—with a corresponding sentiment that gold was growing increasingly scarce and increasingly desirable.

The problem is not, simply, that the private sector in many countries regards gold as the appropriate form in which to invest its savings (in some countries this is traditionally the case, but in others investors are taking an "intelligent" view of the future course of the price of gold in relation to other prices). At least as significant, perhaps, is the tendency for national authorities to seek to concentrate increasingly their official reserve assets on gold. It is not so much that in the very recent past there have been massive conversions of official assets from currency holdings to gold; it has been also become increasingly noticeable that nations are now regarding gold as the least liquid of their reserve assets, with the result that when they begin to run deficits, their first thought is to preserve their gold stock.

One reaction to this situation is the argument that the system needs to be changed. This is argued with his habitual lucidity, by Mr. Bernstein in chapter IV, who points out that the *relative* scarcity of gold will become even greater after the SDR scheme is implemented. Mr. Bernstein's proposal is that henceforth the absolute amount of foreign exchange reserves should be pegged at its present level, the future growth of official liquidity should be looked after by the creation of SDRs—which should be kept within conservative limits to start with—but that special steps should be taken to assure that central banks regard all reserve assets—whether gold, currency or SDRs—as equivalent. To assure the balanced use of all reserve assets in international settlements, he suggests, it will require a rule whereby deficit countries make their settlements according to the exact proportions in which they hold the various forms of reserve assets, and that the surplus countries should accept payment accordingly.

Others, while agreeing that there is a long-term stabilization problem, would be inclined to put more emphasis on a better payments equilibrium, particularly of the reserve currency countries, as an essential prerequisite for the solution of this problem.

The *remedies* proposed for the problems of imbalance and instability differ considerably from each other, and choice between them must depend on how one interprets the nature of the problem. None of the contributors disagrees that, whether or not the rules of the gold exchange system need changing, better adjustment policies would help and should be expected. Within the framework of the OECD Working Party No. 3 is the task of trying to ensure that the adjustment policies of individual countries are mutually reinforcing rather than competitive, and this entails consideration of the balance of payments structures at which individual countries are aiming. Discussion of the mutual compatibility of individual aims immediately brings substantial difficulties to light. For example, many of the major countries are today extremely distant from the positions they aim at, both from the point of view of their overall balances and the current capital structure. And if the reserve currency countries together are seeking to run surpluses, which countries are willing—and to what extent—to run deficits? Not least important, in this respect, is the question whether, in total, the aims of the industrialized countries will result in an adequate growth of capital exports to developing countries—a point which Mr. Márquez touches upon in his contribution. It is this question of total capital outflow which raises in particularly acute form the interdependence of countries' aims and policies if a satisfactory result for the world as a whole is to be achieved. For example, the United Kingdom has decided to reduce its net capital exports to help the necessary strengthening of its position, and not to rely solely on the improvement of its current account. This might well be appropriate, but would require, at the same time, that capital exports by other industrialized countries should be increased so that the flow to developing countries continued to grow.

The possible rôle of *SDR creation* and in particular the first implementation of SDRs have also to be judged in the light of the adjustment thought to be needed. Opinions on the scheme vary with the extent to which emphasis is put on the need to change the international monetary system or the need to improve adjustment policies. Perhaps two extreme views can be distinguished. One view is that the system requires more or less immediate reserve creation, because without it there is little hope of achieving better adjustment policies. And here there may be disagreement with Mr. Bernstein's suggestion that, at the beginning, creation should be modest; it can also be argued that creation of a large amount is required to ensure the credibility of the system. At the other extreme, however, it is argued that the creation of reserves must depend on prior progress towards better adjustment. The real process of adjusting disequilibrium positions, according to this argument, is only just beginning now. The creation of SDRs will not help deficit countries to adjust, and could even do the opposite, and some doubt might be expressed as to the effect that creation might have on the policies of the surplus countries. The premature creation of SDRs might itself effectively destroy the credibility of the SDR system as a whole. Perhaps a third attitude should also be distinguished here. Mr. Gilbert has suggested that, in considering the sufficiency of international liquidity, attention should be paid not simply to the future needs of the world, but also to a backlog of reserve creation which exists today and needs to be made good.

Perhaps it is possible to combine some elements from both the two extreme views which I have just outlined. Even if SDR creation in the near future might carry some disadvantages, in the sense of removing some of the sense of urgency for deficit countries to adjust their positions, it might confer advantages which moved at least compensate. It is surely arguable that the effect of SDR creation on the policies of surplus countries would be favourable, in the sense that it would remove some inhibitions which, in the future, could cause some of them to pursue policies which fall short of the ideal from the point of view of sustainable international equilibrium. But if one was thus to seek some reasonable balance between the contradictory arguments to which I have referred, considerable weight should, perhaps, be attached to the view that the first creation of SDRs should be a modest one, so as not to risk widespread suspicion about the inflationary effects of the change of system and doubts as to the status of "paper-gold". In discussing the problem of SDR implementation one touches upon the wellknown but still urgent need for tools for analysing the world's reserve needs.

I would now like to give a few personal reactions to some of the proposals for the more fundamental *changing of the present system*.

First, to help improve the adjustment process a more flexible exchange rate system is suggested. It is very useful, in such meetings, for alternatives to the present system of movable fixed rates to be discussed. It is clearly short-sighted to persist in a system without, from time to time, reviewing how it has served our purpose and how far possible alternative systems would, on balance, confer advantages or disadvantages. But decisions to change such a system require serious consideration of a complex series of issues and are unlikely to be taken in a hurry. My own view is that the case for change is, so far, not strong. A more flexible exchange rate system could not be a substitute for good internal adjustment policies and the possible disadvantages this system could entail for international trade and capital movements have carefully to be traced. It should be noted, moreover, that the introduction of more flexible rates would create a problem of decision-making, as market intervention—now only a matter of technique—would become a matter of policy of great importance, both nationally and internationally.

Second, various proposals are put forward to make the system more stable after a decision to create additional liquidity. I have already referred to Mr. Bernstein's proposals for a rule to ensure the equitable use of all types of reserve assets, leading to the establishment of a Reserve Settlement Account in the IMF. I find there is much that attracts me in the Bernstein proposals as a means of doing away with some of the existing causes of instability, in particular with the growth of official sterling and dollar balances. Of primary importance, under the present system, is to maintain the convertibility of the reserve currencies, the alternative to which might be disintegration into currency blocks. The Bernstein proposals envisage countries agreeing to abandon gold as an official liquid asset. Before pronouncing on the desirability of such a change in the system, we ought perhaps first to consider how far it is politically realistic to expect countries to abandon this amount of sovereignty over the composition of their reserves in the near future. Moreover, dollar and sterling balances are not only monetary reserves, but also international debts. So possible arrangements entail not only monetary but also important political problems. Perhaps last September's Basle Facility to deal with fluctuations in the sterling balances of sterling countries may be a good example of useful international cooperation to this end, consisting as it does of international action to guarantee the dollar value of part of the sterling holdings in exchange for individual guarantees by sterling countries to hold certain minimum proportions of their reserves in pounds.

Mr. Márquez—in chapter V—criticizes the SDR scheme as anti-social in the sense that it fails to provide the special privileges that the developing countries should receive in the international monetary game. The less-developed countries, he says, have more need of reserves than the industrialized ones, and he would therefore have preferred a scheme whereby all the new liquidity created would have been allocated to the less-developed. There may be a very good case to made out concerning the special reserve needs of developing countries. But I still feel that it is very important not to confuse reserve creation with development aid. The case for steering towards the developing countries an important proportion of the increase in real resources is clear, urgent and widely accepted. But additional liquidity is not necessarily the same as additional real resources, and one needs to look rather closely at any scheme in which there would be a risk that an important part of any liquidity created was immediately translated into a higher demand for goods and services.

I would also like to draw attention to the very interesting chapter that Professors Veltruský and Petrivalský have contributed about the *relationship between the Comecon countries and the IMF countries*. They clearly point up the difficulties, but put forward important ideas concerning the effect which particular decisions by the IMF countries on exchange rate systems and credit creation would have on economic relationships between the two sets of countries. The role of the Comecon countries in the international monetary system seems mainly to depend on future developments within this group. The problems these countries are facing are in some respects, I think, similar to ours at the time of the European Payments Union. I hope we shall be able to follow up the many interesting points made in the course of our discussions.

Finally, I would like to refer to the *International Institutions and the Adjustment Process*, on which Dr. Russell has contributed a chapter. The OECD, and its Working Party No. 3 to which Dr. Russell devotes much attention, are not, of course, the only institutions operating in this field. Other institutions are very important—the Monetary Committee of the EEC and the BIS; and the IMF, on which Mr. Márquez has some stimulating and provocative comments.

The strength of the International Monetary Fund, resides of course in the fact that the Fund is a source of additional liquidity to countries in balance of payments difficulties. On top of this has been built a system of consultation with all countries centred on the practice of thorough *annual* consultations between officials of each countries and a team drawn from the Fund staff. In practice most attention is inevitably paid to the deficit countries. And, in practice, though all decisions have formally to be taken by the Executive Board consisting of country representatives, the initiative falls very largely to the Fund staff. This is not something I point out with regret: on the contrary, it is a strength.

The methods of working of OECD in general—and of Working Party No. 3 in particular—have many points of contrast. First, the OECD has no (or practically no) funds at its disposal: discussions therefore are not directly geared to financial decisions—though the fact that the same countries will be involved in decisions taken in the context of the IMF or the Group of Ten (GAB) inevitably has its influence. Second, the idea of "confrontation"—mutual examination of each country's policies by representatives of other member countries—has deep roots in the OECD, going back to the early post-war years when European countries got into the habit of examining each other's affairs as part and parcel of the allocation of Marshall Aid and mutual assistance for post-war recovery. As a result, the role played by national representatives is probably in practice larger—even though the contribution of the OECD staff is essential and valuable: this is reflected for instance in the senior level at which countries are represented in Working Party No. 3. Another feature which applies in particular to the Working Party is that the process is a continuous one, *not* centred on a routine of annual examinations. It tries to see the problem as a whole, involving all countries not one at a time, and to give equal attention to surplus and deficit countries.

I think both the OECD and the IMF methods of work have their strong points. And since there is need to strengthen the process of international consultation as far as possible, there is need to see the two methods as mutually reinforcing, and part of one operation. Among the questions to be discussed are the following:

i. Do we keep a sufficiently searching and continuous watch on the international adjustment process?

ii. No discussion—national or international—is likely to be fruitful unless the discussion has been prepared. Conclusions are not arrived at by a group unless proposals are made to them. Is there then a need for the Secretariat of international bodies to play a larger role in making proposals for adjustments of policy—and possibly making them at an earlier stage and in a more continuous way than at present?

iii. Are there some aspects of the adjustment process that are unduly neglected at the moment in this respect? Dr. Russell, I notice, has some observations on the taboo on mentioning exchange rates: it has, he says, been held to be "diplomatically impolite to suggest to another nation that it alter its exchange rate."

Concluding this short introduction I would like to stress once again the usefulness of reviewing the existing patterns continuously and carefully and look for renovation and improvement. I hold the opinion that we have to aim at an evolution of the gold exchange standard into an increasingly rational international monetary system, managed by collective decisions of governments. It is the basic philosophy of the International Monetary Fund and of its new Special Drawing Rights Scheme. Indeed, considerable progress towards more meaningful international monetary cooperation in the interests of the world economy has already been made in recent years. The regular meetings at a high level have led to more familiarity with the international aspects of the problems and have appeared to be increasingly useful. There is, for instance, much more agreement than ever before on the aims of economic policy and on the importance of their international compatibility, and there is a growing recognition that adjustment can be effectively made only by using all available instruments of economic policy, monetary policy included. The name of one of the sponsoring institutions of this publication reminds us of the late President John F. Kennedy. On June 25th 1963 he said at Frankfort: "The great face nations of the world must take control of their monetary problems if those problems are not to control them." The face nations have, I think, been able to take control of the monetary problems on some crucial points. But we all know that there is much room for further improvement.

Chapter II

THE PRESENT IMBALANCE IN INTERNATIONAL PAYMENTS

by *Milton Gilbert*

Introduction

The events since the second half of 1967 reveal clearly that the payments situation has been showing increasing fragility and a tendency to be crisis-prone. First, the sterling crisis in the second half of 1967 led to a devaluation of the pound on 18th November of that year, without it becoming evident in the subsequent months that sterling had been put on a firm footing. This was followed by two speculative buying waves in the gold market in November-December 1967 and in March 1968 which reached such large proportions that on 17th March the gold pool gave up its efforts to hold down the market price to near the $ 35 level. The social disturbances in France in May-June 1968 gave a shock to confidence in the French franc, which resulted in very large reserve losses and deterioration in the balance-of-payments position. Then, rumours of revaluation of the Deutsche Mark produced a large flow of liquid funds to Germany in August, and in November a more massive movement involving mainly the Deutsche Mark, the French franc and sterling caused a crisis which required the principal exchange markets in Europe to be closed. In this chapter I have aimed to present the facts on present international imbalances.

There are six countries principally involved in present imbalances, the substance of which is to be found in the current-account positions of these countries. (Switzerland also was in substantial overall surplus in 1968, but mainly because of capital inflows.) On the one hand, there are the very large current-account surpluses in Germany, Italy and Japan, and on the other hand, the substantial current-account deficits in France and the United Kingdom. In addition, there is the inadequate current-account surplus in the United States. For the year 1968 as a whole the current-account imbalances were larger than in 1967.

In three out of these six countries—Germany, Italy and the United States—the current-account position was either partially or wholly offset in 1968 by abnormally large capital movements and changes in the external positions of the banks, so that the movements in their reserves last year did not reflect the underlying imbalances. This was particularly the case in Italy, where there was no change in reserves, taking the year as a whole, and in the United States where the net reserve position showed a marked statistical improvement. In France and the United Kingdom, on the other hand, reserves fell by much more than the current-account deficit, France having had—in addition—a large flight of capital and the United Kingdom both some long-term capital outflow and a further switching out of sterling by non-residents.

It is not difficult to see the nature of the external changes that are needed in these countries to bring about a better balance in international payments. On the one hand, France, the United Kingdom and the United States all need improvements on current account sufficient to enable them to cover normal outflows of long-term capital and, in addition, the United Kingdom needs a current surplus large enough to enable it to begin paying off the external debts it has incurred since 1964. On the other hand, Germany, Italy and Japan need to reduce their current surpluses to a level that is more in line with a normal volume of capital exports. The improvement needed in the current accounts of France, the United Kingdom and the United States is at least of the order of $ 7-8 billion; but, if the other three countries are to be left with reasonable current-account surpluses, not much more than half of this improvement can come from them.

It seems clear, therefore, that the full correction of the French, British and US positions would necessarily have an appreciable adverse effect on the rest of the world's current balance of payments. And this effect would be bound to be rather painful so long as the international monetary system remains in a situation where the net creation of new monetary reserves is, as it has been for some years, rather small. In other words, the adjustment problems of these countries are very much complicated by the existence of what must be called a disequilibrium of the monetary system as such. This question is taken up in the final section of the paper.

Germany

The strength of Germany's current balance of payments has in recent months been the feature of the existing international payments difficulties that has attracted the most attention, to the point where it has twice led to large-scale international speculation in favour of the Deutsche Mark. It therefore seems appropriate to begin this survey with a look at the recent external situation of Germany (see table I).

For the year 1968 Germany's current external balance showed a surplus of $ 2.9 billion, including a trade surplus of $ 4.6 billion. Both the trade surplus and the current-account surplus were somewhat higher than in 1967 despite an acceleration in the growth of GNP between the two years from less than 1 to 9 per cent. The strong growth of internal demand produced a rise of $ 2.8 billion, or over 15 per cent, in imports. And this rise would have been even larger if it had not been for a 2 per cent fall in import prices. But at the same time exports rose by $ 3.1 billion.

Some part of the 1968 increase in exports was artificial and reflected accelerated deliveries of goods at the end of the year just before the reduced tax rebate on exports came into effect. But even without this special factor the foreign trade surplus would have been nearly as big as in 1967. The main factor that held it up, therefore, was the strong underlying demand for German exports, which was a reflection of the general strengthening of demand in the rest of the world during 1968. Total imports into all industrial countries except Germany in fact rose by 13 per cent between the middle two quarters of 1967 and 1968, as against a rise of less than 6 per cent the year before. So far as Germany is concerned, there were three important sources of extra export demand in 1968: the rest of the Common Market, whose imports from Germany rose by 17 per cent, as against 9 per cent in 1967; the United States, where imports from Germany rose by 38 per cent, as against less than 10 per cent in 1967; and the United Kingdom, whose imports from Germany were up by 16 per cent, as against 11 per cent in 1967.

Owing mainly to the easy monetary policy of the Bundesbank, the whole of the 1968 current external surplus was offset by long-term capital exports. The overall payments surplus of $ 1 billion therefore simply

Table I

GERMANY: BALANCE OF PAYMENTS

		1964
Exports (f.o.b.)...		16,230
Imports (c.i.f.)		14,710
Trade balance...		1,520
Services	— 180	
Unilateral transfers	—1,300	
Invisibles (net)		—1,480
Current account		40
Long-term capital		
Private...	90	
Official	— 310	
Total (net)...		— 220
Basic balance		— 180
Debt prepayments		—
Non-monetary short-term capital (net)		— 215
Errors and omissions		480
Overall balance (= changes in monetary items)...........................		85
Commercial banks' net position		— 25
Net official assets		110

reflected the net inflows of short-term capital. During the second and third quarters of 1968 the basic balance of payments was in fact in deficit, long-term capital outflows having been larger than the current-account surplus. But the size and persistence of the trade surplus, plus the fact that the high level of capital exports was dependent on the easy monetary policy of the authorities, gave rise to fears that the basic balance could swing into substantial surplus. These fears, against the background of

1965	1966	1967	1968
in millions of US dollars (rounded)			
17,910	20,160	21,760	24,885
17,610	18,170	17,545	20,295
300	1,990	4,215	4,590
— 345	— 355	— 220	45
—1,585	—1,560	—1,565	—1,715
—1,930	—1,915	—1,785	—1,670
—1,630	75	2,430	2,920
555	455	— 445	—2,545
— 320	— 350	— 360	— 345
235	105	— 805	—2,890
—1,395	180	1,625	30
—	— 235	—	—
530	440	35	335
650	110	— 360	580
— 215	495	1,300	945
110	145	1,205	— 790
— 325	350	95	1,735

uncertainties about other currencies, were the essential factor behind the rumours of a possible DM revaluation that brought about the large inflows of funds into Germany in August-September and again in November 1968.

During the first of these episodes the bulk of the inflow was rapidly rechannelled by the Bundesbank to the market by means of forward swap operations at rates highly favourable to the commercial banks. As a result, the increase in Germany's reserves during September, which otherwise would have been something approaching $ 2 billion, was limited to only $ 300 million. The inflow in the early weeks of November was on an even larger scale. Despite the Bundesbank's efforts—again through its forward swap policy—to re-export funds through the banks, the reserves rose by $ 2.4 billion in the first three weeks of November, including $ 1¾ billion in the last few days alone.

In response to this immense pressure and to the strain it imposed on other currencies, mainly the French franc and the pound sterling, the principal European exchange markets were closed down on 20th November and the Ministers and central-bank Governors of the Group of Ten met in Bonn to discuss the situation. The German authorities had announced their decision not to revalue the Deutsche Mark. Instead, they introduced a reduction from 11 to 7 per cent in the tax rebates for exports, together with a corresponding downward change in the border taxes on imports. At the same time they took various measures designed to reverse the inflow of funds and to discourage possible similar inflows in the future.

The decision of the German authorities not to revalue the Deutsche Mark last November, whatever may have been the political considerations involved, is not hard to understand in the light of the balance of payments both at that time and as it had developed over recent years.

In the first place, as already mentioned, the basic balance of payments was actually in deficit at that time. To have changed the rate would therefore have appeared as a response to short-term capital movements rather than to a situation of fundamental disequilibrium.

Secondly, it was not so long since the current balance of payments had been in substantial deficit and it appeared that the subsequent improvement had been mainly due to the influence of cyclical factors, both in Germany and elsewhere. Thus, excess internal demand had produced a current-account deficit of $ 1.6 billion in 1965; and, with imports soaring, there was even a deficit on trade account by the third quarter of 1965. The tightening of monetary policy in 1965 and early 1966 produced a fairly rapid recovery in the current account, to a position of approximate balance in 1966 and a surplus of $ 2.4 billion in 1967. This, however, went hand in hand with a situation in which total domestic demand stopped growing and then actually declined somewhat between mid-1966 and mid-1967. And, although monetary policy shifted to ease in the latter part of 1966, the recovery of domestic activity did not get firmly under way until the latter part of 1967. It was expected, therefore, that in 1968, as the recovery gained momentum, the current surplus would decline substantially, especially as imports in 1967 had been somewhat lower than in 1966. That this did not in fact happen could reasonably be attributed by the German authorities to temporary factors, for which an irreversible action like revaluation would not seem appropriate.

Looking at the whole period from 1964 to 1968, it appears that the changes in Germany's balance of payments were mainly related to cyclical fluctuations both in Germany and in other countries. Some competitive advantage was gained from the recession, as price stability was re-established in Germany while prices rose in several other important countries—Germany's share of world exports having risen from 10.8 to 11.4 per cent between 1965 and 1967. But this would not seem to be the major factor in the recent strength of the balance of payments. Thus, it was not surprising that last November the German authorities felt that a good part of the responsibility for correcting the imbalance lay with other countries—and in particular with France, the United Kingdom and the United States, where the level of imports was giving rise to anxiety.

Following the measures taken in November 1968, there was at once a heavy reflux of funds out of Germany. By the end of January 1969 all the money that had come in during the November crisis had been re-exported and that aspect of the November crisis had been resolved. The impact of the change in border taxes—which in fact amounts to a tem-porary de facto revaluation of the Deutsche Mark so far as foreign trade (except trade in agricultural products, which are governed by EEC regulations) is concerned—will of course not become clear for several months. While its first impact, as already mentioned, was to accelerate the delivery of exports in December 1968, there was a very sharp fall in the trade surplus in January 1969.

What are the prospects for Germany's balance of payments in 1969? Internal economic developments seem certain to be in the direction of bringing about a better balance on current account. Domestic demand is expected to increase strongly, perhaps by 7-8 per cent, with both in-vestment and consumption rising by more than in 1968. As, however, real output is not likely to expand so fast, demand pressures on produc-tive resources and prices seem likely to become evident. Indeed, by the middle of March some increase on the anticipated rate of price rise was already apparent, causing the government to prepare a mild package of fiscal restraint. The expected increase in the pressure of internal demand, together with some cooling off in other important countries and the reaction from the acceleration of exports at the end of 1968, could pro-duce a marked fall in the current-account surplus—perhaps to a level of about $ 1.5 billion.

This would be, of course, a rather large current-account surplus in con-ditions of high internal demand pressure. It could probably be offset by capital exports, provided that monetary policy remained fairly easy. But if domestic conditions should develop in a way that called forth a tight monetary policy, capital exports could drop sharply and an overall pay-ments surplus could re-emerge. Interest rates early in 1969 were edging upwards, although this was largely in response to the pressure from rates abroad which was transmitted through heavy foreign issues on the Ger-man market in January and February. Furthermore, it was announced in late February that the Bundesbank would no longer support the bond market through purchases on its own account.

A good deal will depend on the flexibility with which fiscal and mone-tary policy are combined in Germany as productive resources come under pressure. It could even be argued that the decision not to revalue implies toleration of some price increase. But much also will depend on the success of the efforts now being made in France, the United Kingdom and the United States to improve their current balances of payments.

Italy

Balance-of-payments developments in Italy have been overshadowed by the attention recently focused on the German situation. In fact, Italy's balance of payments has been in surplus since the spring of 1964 when the crisis that broke out in 1963 was overcome. And from the second quarter of 1964 until the end of 1968 a cumulative overall surplus of $ 4.3 billion was recorded (see Table II).

Looking first at developments in 1968, the already large current-account surplus increased by about 50 per cent, to a figure of $ 2 billion. It is true that long-term capital outflows of $ 1.4 billion offset 70 per cent of the current surplus in 1968 and that the overall surplus of $ 0.6 billion did not give rise to any increase in reserves. But the 1968 long-term capital outflow cannot be regarded as a normal, or as a desirable, permanent feature of the external position.

As in Germany, the size of the current external surplus in 1968 was determined by developments in the foreign trade account. The trade deficit declined between 1967 and 1968 from $ 1.1 to only 0.3 billion, which was an even lower figure than in the recession year of 1965. The 1968 improvement in the foreign trade balance was more marked than in Germany, since it was the result not only of very strong demand for Italian exports but also of a continuing moderate rate of increase in imports. The growth of imports in 1968, measured on the payments basis shown in the table, was maintained at the 1967 figure of 8 per cent. Measured on the basis of the movement of goods, however, the growth of imports slowed down between 1967 and 1968 from just over 14 to just over 4 per cent. At the same time, the growth of total domestic demand, in real terms, fell off from $6\frac{1}{2}$ to 4 per cent. The growth of exports, on the other hand, accelerated from $7\frac{1}{2}$ to 19 per cent. The resumption of expansion in Germany was the biggest single factor in the acceleration of export growth. Italian exports to Germany, which had fallen by $5\frac{1}{2}$ per cent in 1967, rose by nearly 23 per cent last year. Exports to France and the Netherlands also rose faster than in 1967, so that total sales to the

Table II

ITALY: BALANCE OF PAYMENTS*

		1964
Exports (f.o.b.)		5,580
Imports (c.i.f.)		7,070
Trade balance		—1,490
Tourism	825	
Workers' remittances	550	
Other invisibles	440	
Invisibles (net)		1,815
Current account		325
Long-term capital		
Private	430	
Official	35	
Total (net)		465
Basic balance		790
Debt prepayments		—
Non-monetary short-term capital (net)		10
Overall balance (= changes in monetary items)		800
Commercial banks' net position		450
Net official assets		350

* On a cash basis.

Common Market were up by 20 per cent, as against less than 3 per cent in 1967. Furthermore, the growth rate of exports to the United States roughly doubled between the two years, from just over 15 to just under 30 per cent.

The size of Italy's 1968 current surplus therefore owed a lot, though by

1965		1966		1967	1968	
in millions of US dollars (rounded)						
	6,655		7,605	8,170		9,725
	7,130		8,600	9,290		10,040
	— 475		— 995	—1,120		— 315
1,065		1,200		1,125	1,110	
675		730		680	740	
370		470		600	440	
	2,110		2,400	2,405		2,290
	1,635		1,405	1,285		1,975
— 105		— 640		— 875	—1,315	
60		— 40		— 50	— 110	
	— 45		— 680	— 925		—1,425
	1,590		725	360		550
	—		— 145	—		—
	— 15		— 20	15		35
	1,575		560	375		585
	620		390	— 180		720
	955		170	555		— 135

no means all, to demand developments in certain other countries. But 1968 was the fourth successive year in which there had been a very substantial current surplus and the fifth in which the overall payments balance had been in comfortable surplus. And looking at the course of events over the period from 1964 to 1968, the main factor in the persistently high current surplus was undoubtedly the slower rate of growth of domestic demand.

During 1964-67 the average annual growth of real GNP was 4½ per cent, as against 6½ per cent during 1960-63. The origins of this slowing down go back to the payments crisis of 1963 and to the measures taken to deal with it. Between 1962 and 1963 the overall external situation had deteriorated from a position of approximate balance to a deficit of $ 1.2 billion, and during the period October 1963 to March 1964 the overall deficit was running at an annual rate of $ 1.8 billion. The main cause of the crisis lay in a rapid increase of wages, at an annual rate of 15 per cent from mid-1962 to mid-1964. As a result, both consumption and the price level rose rather rapidly and the current balance of payments shifted from a $ 250 million surplus in 1962 to a $ 900 million deficit the following year. Late in 1963 and again early in 1964 the authorities took corrective measures, especially by monetary restraint, and by the second quarter of 1964 the balance of payments was back in surplus. For the year 1964 the current balance showed a moderate surplus, of $ 325 million, and capital imports brought the overall surplus up to $ 800 million.

The balance-of-payments crisis was therefore rather quickly over. But the internal effects proved more lasting. Total domestic demand, after having expanded on average by 7½ per cent a year during 1960-63, showed practically no further increase in either 1964 or 1965, with sharp falls in investment in both years. Unemployment, which between 1960 and 1963 had fallen from 4 to 2½ per cent, had by 1966 practically regained the 1960 level; employment in industry (excluding building), which had gone up by 6½ per cent during 1960-63, fell back by nearly 4½ per cent between 1963 and 1966; and the building industry's labour force, after increasing by 17½ per cent during 1960-64, declined over the two following years by about 10 per cent. It was, therefore, not surprising that the external surplus which had re-emerged towards the middle of 1964 continued through 1965 and 1966—though in the latter year it fell off quite considerably as imports picked up and a rather large volume of capital exports developed in response to the liquid state of the economy.

With the recession giving way to renewed expansion, real GNP increased by an annual average of $5\frac{1}{2}$ per cent during 1966-68, slightly more than the figure envisaged in the National Plan for 1966-70. The upswing, however, did not bring the economy back to full employment. Unemployment declined, but in 1968 still averaged $3\frac{1}{2}$ per cent; the labour force engaged in industry, except building, rose again but in the third quarter of 1968 was no higher than it had been, on the average, in 1963. And towards the end of 1968 total employment in building was still 5 per cent below the 1963 level. In fact, the recent rate of increase of real GNP has remained some way below the $6\frac{1}{2}$ per cent annual average for 1960-63. And, in particular, gross domestic capital formation, the principal victim of the recession, had by 1968 scarcely more than regained its 1963 level.

There was little change in the balance-of-payments position in 1967, despite the German recession and the cost of the late-1966 floods. Then, in 1968, the current surplus rose again sharply as foreign demand strengthened simultaneously with a renewed slackening of domestic demand. In the latter half of 1968 the authorities decided to supplement their easy monetary policy with more direct measures to stimulate the economy. These measures were concentrated on trying to accelerate the growth of investment. In the public sector existing investment plans, the execution of which had lagged behind expectations, are to be speeded up and at the same time a railway modernisation programme is to be embarked upon. In the private sector tax incentives for non-agricultural investment have been introduced. More recently a bill providing for quite substantial increases in old-age and retirement pensions in 1969—the cost of which over the next ten years is estimated at nearly $ 13 billion, beginning with a figure of over $ 800 million (equal to over $1\frac{1}{2}$ per cent of total private consumption)—has been put before the Italian Parliament.

The present structure of the Italian balance of payments, with a very large surplus on current account and long-term capital exports that in 1968 were equal to 2 per cent of GNP, is recognised by the Italian authorities as inappropriate. Indeed, the National Plan for 1966-70 explicitly envisaged a decline in the current external surplus. As a very large surplus on invisible account has probably to be taken as a datum, any substantial reduction of the current surplus can come about only through an increase in the foreign trade deficit. On the export side, it certainly seems unlikely that the 1968 rate of growth will continue for long. But even if it slowed down quite considerably, there could still be a fairly large current surplus unless at the same time the growth of imports speeded up. The impact on internal demand of recent policy measures, and especially of the attempts to stimulate public investment programmes, is not easy to guess at. On balance it seems likely to take some time before the recent pattern of the balance of payments is very greatly modified.

Japan

Japan's balance of payments showed a remarkable improvement between 1967 and 1968, from an overall deficit of $ 570 million to an overall surplus of $ 1.100 million. Part of this improvement resulted from the effects on imports and on the capital account of the restrictive measures taken by the Japanese authorities in mid-1967 when the external position was in rather heavy deficit. In addition, developments in other countries during 1968 were favourable to a rapid growth of Japan's exports (see Table III).

The biggest change between 1967 and 1968 was in the foreign trade sector, where the surplus went up from $ 1.2 to 2.5 billion. The greater part of this reflected the acceleration of export growth from about 6 per cent—easily the lowest rate of growth observed for some years—to 25 per cent in 1968. Japan benefited very substantially from the 1968 upsurge of imports into the United States, its largest trading partner. Japanese sales to the United States, which had shown hardly any increase in 1967, rose by 36 per cent in 1968. This was considerably more than the 1968 rise of total US imports, which amounted to 23 per cent. The other very large rise in Japanese exports last year occurred in Southeast Asia. Sales to this group of countries, which in total are almost as large as those to the United States, rose by 23 per cent last year.

On the other side of the foreign trade balance, the growth of imports slowed down between 1967 and 1968 from 23 to 13 per cent. The restrictive monetary and fiscal measures taken by the Japanese authorities in 1967 to cool off the boom and to improve the balance of payments did not produce any very marked reduction in overall growth. Real GNP rose during 1968 by just on 14 per cent. But the tight money policy did lead to a business inventory adjustment in the first half of 1968. As a

Table III

JAPAN: BALANCE OF PAYMENTS

	1966	1967	1968
	in millions of US dollars (rounded)		
Exports (f.o.b.)	9,640	10,230	12,750
Imports (f.o.b.)	7,365	9,070	10,220
Trade balance	2,275	1,160	2,530
Invisibles (net)	—1,025	—1,350	—1,480
Current account	1,250	— 190	1,050
Long-term capital (net)	— 810	— 800	— 240
Basic balance	440	— 990	810
Short-term capital (net)	— 120	420	290
Overall balance (= changes in monetary items)	320	— 570	1,100
Commercial banks' net position	385	— 510	240
Net official assets	— 65	— 60	860

result, the 13 per cent rise in imports during 1968 was less than the increase of almost 18 per cent in domestic mining and manufacturing production.

After taking into account some further increase in the net deficit on services account (including unilateral transfers), the effect of the big improvement in the foreign trade balance was to swing the current account of the balance of payments from a deficit of $ 0.2 billion to a surplus of over $ 1 billion. And on top of that net outflows of long-term capital declined rather sharply from $ 0.8 to 0.2 billion. Here, too, the tight monetary policy introduced in 1967 and continued into 1968 had a considerable effect. In particular, it led to an increase of about $ 450 million in longer-term borrowing by Japanese corporations from financial institutions in other countries. The capital account also benefited in 1968 from a rise of about $ 150 million in foreign purchases of Japanese securities, the prices of which had fallen to rather low levels in the course of 1967.

The size of Japan's overall surplus in 1968 appears to have been rather exceptional. Exports are hardly likely to continue rising at 25 per cent a year or imports to continue rising less fast than industrial production. Nor will the capital account necessarily continue to show net outflows as small as those of 1968. The immediate prospect therefore is for some reduction in the overall payments surplus. At the same time the remarkable stability of Japanese wholesale prices, especially in the export sectors, points to the underlying strength of Japan's position in international trade.

Switzerland

The strength of the Swiss franc has traditionally been maintained without the balance of payments having shown particularly large surpluses. From such information as is available, however, it appears that between 1967 and 1968 there was a very marked rise in the overall external surplus, measured by the changes in net official monetary assets and in the short-term foreign position of the banks, from only $ 0.1 billion to rather more than $ 1 billion. Whereas in the countries so far discussed the surpluses arose essentially out of current-account developments, in the case of Switzerland the emergence of a large overall surplus in 1968 was mainly due to capital movements.

The trade deficit declined by $ 130 million in 1968, exports having risen by 14½ per cent and imports by just over 9 per cent. The strong growth of exports principally reflected the impact of demand in Common Market countries, notably Germany, as well as in certain overseas markets. In addition to the improvement on trade account, the invisible surplus, and in particular net income on investment account, increased during 1968. Altogether, the current-account surplus is estimated to have gone up by some $ 200 million to about $ 450 million. The remainder of the overall surplus for 1968, therefore, and most of the change in the overall balance between the two years must have arisen out of a rather large net inflow of non-monetary capital. It seems likely that two factors were mainly responsible for this development—the French crisis and an increase in the export of capital from Italy in the form of banknotes.

If allowance is made for the effects of end-year transfers of foreign exchange from the commercial banks to the Swiss National Bank, it appears that practically the whole of Switzerland's overall external surplus in 1968 was re-exported at short term through the commercial banks. If, however, the domestic monetary situation were to tighten, there could be a considerable rise in Switzerland's reserves.

France

In most of the other countries discussed in this chapter the external imbalance emerged rather gradually and usually originated in a change in relative demand conditions at home and abroad. The deficit in the French balance of payments in 1968 was different in both respects. It derived for the most part from a sudden massive flight from the franc which was in anticipation of rather than in response to an adverse shift in

France's international position following the social unrest in May (see Table IV).

Table IV

FRANCE: BALANCE OF PAYMENTS WITH NON-FRANC COUNTRIES*

		1965
Exports (f.o.b.)		8,265
Imports (f.o.b.)		7,935
Trade balance		+ 330
Investment income	+ 85	
Tourism	— 30	
Other private services	+ 295	
Government	+ 55	
Foreign workers' remittances	— 275	
Invisibles (net)		+ 130
Current account		+ 460
Long-term capital (net)		+ 290
Private investment abroad	— 175	
Private investment in France	+ 535	
Official capital	— 70	
Basic balance		+ 750
Debt prepayments		— 180
Non-monetary short-term capital (net)		— 90
Multilateral settlements, balancing item, etc.		+ 480
Overall balance		+ 960
Commercial banks' net position		+ 255
Net official assets		+ 705

* On a cash basis.

This is not to say that there had been no decline in France's external position in the preceding years. The current-account surplus with non-

1966	1967	1968 (tentative estimates)
in millions of US dollars (rounded)		
8,985	10,150	11,250
9,015	10,000	11,900
− 30	+ 150	(− 650)
+ 90	+ 105	..
+ 10	− 5	..
+ 260	+ 250	..
+ 40	− 125	..
− 330	− 365	..
+ 70	− 140	(− 800)
+ 40	+ 10	(−1,450)
+ 80	+ 265	(− 300)
− 215	− 305	..
+ 370	+ 615	..
− 75	− 45	..
+ 120	+ 275	(−1,750)
− 70	&minus;	&minus;
− 115	− 315	(−1,400)
+ 370	+ 5	
+ 305	− 35	(−3,150)
− 80	− 370	(+ 500)
+ 385	+ 335	(−3,650)

franc countries, which amounted to $ 460 million in 1965, on a cash basis, had just about disappeared by 1967, due to a weakening on both trade and invisible accounts. The decline in the trade surplus over these two years (which was rather more pronounced on a transactions basis) was largely a result of the easing of total demand in foreign countries in 1966-67, reflected in the slow increase in French exports. The decline in the invisible balance, on the other hand, from a $ 130 million surplus to a slightly larger deficit, seemed to be of a more structural nature. It followed a previous deterioration from a net invisible surplus of $ 550 million in 1960, which had been due mainly to rising French travel expenditure and increasing remittances by immigrant workers. Although the balance on tourist spending showed no further decline after 1965, the rising trend of workers' remittances continued, and in 1967 there was a deterioration on government account related to the withdrawal of NATO headquarters and of US military bases from France.

There was, therefore, some underlying weakening in France's external position over these years. However, the net inflow of long-term capital, which has typically accompanied France's current-account surplus during the 1960s, continued in 1967, and the basic balance of payments remained in surplus to the extent of $ 275 million. There was a small overall deficit in that year of $ 35 million, associated with an outflow of short-term funds, but this outflow could not be regarded as a permanent feature of the accounts. Moreover, the 1967 deficit followed years of large surplus which had led to the accumulation of some $ 7 billion of official reserves.

Thus, by the beginning of 1968 the French surplus position of the earlier 1960s had been relieved, but the overall balance was probably still in moderate underlying surplus. Although concern was expressed in some quarters about the effect on French industry of the final stage of EEC internal tariff reductions scheduled for mid-1968, there was no question of external weakness being an actual problem at that time.

Assessment of the change which occurred in the course of last year is made difficult by the absence as yet of any official balance-of-payments data. I am, therefore, obliged to rely upon my own very tentative estimates which are shown in the table. The overall deficit for the year was something over $ 3 billion. I would attribute rather over half of this, say $ 1¾ billion, to a basic deficit and the remainder essentially to a flight of non-monetary short-term capital. In addition, there was an outflow of funds through the commercial banking system of over $ 0.5 billion, so that net official assets fell by some $ 3.7 billion.

It must be emphasised that the confidence crisis not only was responsible for the flight of short-term capital but also was the main factor behind the large basic deficit. The previous net import of long-term capital almost certainly was turned into a substantial outflow, probably mainly because of a swing in the portfolio balance caused by anticipation of exchange rate adjustments. On current account a major reason for the weakening on net invisibles appears to have been higher remittances by foreign workers, who transferred accumulated savings as well as current earnings; and much of the decline in the trade balance (on a cash basis) derived from an adverse shift in terms of payment.

Abstracting from these confidence effects, and from the severe temporary loss of tourist income due to the strikes and uncertainties, the underlying deterioration in France's external position in 1968 would appear relatively small. In particular, customs data show a decline in the trade balance of only $ 265 million for the year as a whole. Nevertheless, the position had worsened more seriously by the end of 1968. In the fourth quarter imports, on a customs basis, were just under 20 per cent above their pre-strike level and exports 8 per cent greater, so that the trade deficit was at an annual rate of about $ 2¼ billion compared with little more than $ ½ billion in the first four months of 1968. The developing weakness in the trade balance was exaggerated by the unfavourable effect of the currency uncertainty on trade transactions themselves, particularly in the fourth quarter, and by artificially high imports from Germany in December. Basically, though, it reflected the rapid rise in economic activity after the strikes and probably, too, a deterioration in France's competitive position.

The Grenelle settlement in May 1968 provided for a general 10 per cent increase in wages together with a larger rise in minimum rates and higher social security benefits. This abrupt stimulus to consumer spending came at a time when economic policy was already directed towards more rapid expansion. Partly because there was initial under-utilisation of capacity, domestic output was able to respond strongly to the increase in demand, and by the end of 1968 the level of industrial production was 10 per cent higher than a year before. Even so, it was inevitable that there should be an accompanying rise in imports.

The growth of industrial output was achieved very largely through higher labour productivity. Although there were reports of skilled-labour shortage and advertised vacancies increased, unemployment at end-1968 was somewhat higher than a year before and total employment decreased. This enabled a part of the sharp rise in wage costs to be absorbed, and prices were also held back by direct government intervention. Nevertheless, industrial wholesale prices increased by 6 per cent between April and December. Much of the effect on export prices was offset by subsidies (amounting to 6 per cent of wage costs from June to November and 3 per cent thereafter) and by cheap export credit. And, although the subsidies were abolished and export credit rates increased early this year, a comparable effect has been achieved by the change in business taxes, replacing payroll tax by a higher value-added tax which is recoverable on exports. This change equally has the effect of raising the final price of imports. Despite these measures, it seems certain that France's international price competitive position, which was probably improving early in 1968, has since worsened significantly.

The present outlook for the French balance of payments is particularly obscure. The outflow of funds was effectively halted in November by the reimposition of rigorous exchange controls on transactions by residents and by the move to curb economic expansion through monetary and fiscal policy. The foreign exchange regulations also induced a reduction in the banks' net foreign position which in the three months December-February made possible a significant rise in the reserves and at the same time some reduction in short-term official borrowing. It seems unlikely, however, that any very large voluntary return of funds will occur until the present weakness on current transactions has been demonstrably over-come.

The invisible balance could improve considerably. Tourist earnings should recover and workers' remittances should fall back to a more normal level. Also, France will benefit from larger payments by the EEC Agricultural Fund. The likely development on trade account is harder to foresee. Domestic demand is expected to rise more moderately following the change in economic policy in November; but how much more mod-erately will depend upon the outcome of the wage negotiations in March and upon whether or not the level of unemployment gives rise to demand by the public for stimulative policy measures. At the same time, it may be that demand conditions abroad will be less favourable to French exports than in 1968. Finally, the extent to which existing and foreseeable cost pressures will be transmitted in a further rise of prices remains uncertain, even with the tighter price controls now in force. In these conditions it would seem optimistic to anticipate a very rapid improve-ment in the underlying trade balance, although a reaction to the exag-gerated deficit of the fourth quarter of last year may be expected.

United Kingdom

The history of balance-of-payments weakness in the United Kingdom and the background to the devaluation of sterling in November 1967 were rather fully discussed in the BIS Annual Report of 1968 and require no elaboration here. The more current question is why progress towards external recovery over the past year has not been more rapid (see Table V).

The indications are that the basic deficit in 1968, at about $ 1.1 billion, was not significantly less than in 1967. Moreover, the balancing item, which had included a large unrecorded inflow early in 1967, became negative so that the overall balance worsened from a deficit of $ 0.9 billion to one of $ 1.3 billion. At the same time the official financing requirement was again larger than the overall deficit, because of a monetary outflow. A good part of this outflow was related to reserve diversification by sterling-area countries last year, at least until the support arrangement for the sterling-area balances was set up by a group of central banks and the BIS in the autumn. But the fact that private funds withdrawn in anticipation of the parity change did not return to London reflects a persistent lack of confidence fostered by the limited improvement in the basic balance.

There was a reduction in net long-term capital outflows in 1968, from $ 240 to 95 million. This came about through a turnround on official capital account from a net outflow to a net inflow, partly because the capital repayments due at the end of 1968 on the post-war North American loans were deferred. The private long-term capital account

Table V

UNITED KINGDOM: BALANCE OF PAYMENTS

	1967
Seasonally adjusted	
Exports (f.o.b.).	13,880
Imports (f.o.b.)	15,295
Trade balance.	—1,415
Payments for US military aircraft	— 265
Invisibles (net)	+ 635
Current account	—1,045
Long-term capital (net).	— 240
Basic balance	—1,285
Unadjusted	
Basic balance	—1,285
Balancing item	+ 425
Overall balance	— 860

weakened early in the year, when there were heavy purchases by UK residents of foreign, particularly Australian, securities. In the third quarter, however, a few very large transactions related to direct investment in the United Kingdom produced a net inflow on private capital account. Overall, there was nothing to indicate any permanent change in the long-term capital account.

An improvement in the net invisible surplus is of greater longer-term significance. The deficit on government transactions, which had contributed substantially to the weakening of the external position up to 1967, declined somewhat in dollar terms in 1968. And the private invisible surplus, on a steadily rising long-term trend, strengthened quite sharply

		1968		
Year	I	II	III	IV
in millions of US dollars (rounded)				
14,645	3,580	3,445	3,760	3,860
16,295	4,005	3,995	4,125	4,170
—1,650	— 425	— 550	— 365	— 310
— 260	— 55	— 75	— 85	— 45
+ 905	+ 155	+ 305	+ 275	+ 170
—1,005	— 325	— 320	— 175	— 185
— 95	— 325	— 55	+ 460	— 175
—1,100	— 650	— 375	+ 285	— 360
—1,100	— 710	— 250	+ 150	— 290
— 210	— 210	+ 10	+ 35	— 45
—1,310	— 920	— 240	+ 185	— 335

last year with the improvement touching most sections of the accounts. In total, the net surplus on all invisible items rose by some $ 0.3 billion to $ 0.9 billion. While a part of the improvement resulted directly from devaluation, which for example cut the foreign exchange cost of servicing sterling debts, it was nevertheless a permanent gain, and in addition there was an underlying increase in net invisible earnings.

The strengthening on both long-term capital and invisible accounts was not reflected in a fall in the basic deficit. This was because the trade balance, where devaluation was expected to have its major effect, worsened from a deficit of $ 1.4 billion to one of $ 1.65 billion in 1968. In fact, the real worsening in the trade balance was substantially larger than these figures suggest. The 1967 results had been unfavourably affected both by the upsurge of imports following the removal of the surcharge in late 1966 and by delays in exports following the late-1967 dock strikes, whereas early in 1968 the trade balance was favourably affected by the carryover of exports from 1967. The outturn on trade account was, therefore, disappointing and it is on the trade balance that the position of sterling will continue to depend.

The trouble did not seem to lie mainly with exports, which responded rather well to the new situation. After rough allowance for special influences, the volume of exports in 1968 was some 10 per cent greater than the year before—double its average growth rate in recent years. Moreover, the underlying rise in the export volume in the course of 1968 was considerably larger. This result owed much to the strength of total demand in overseas markets and was surpassed by several other industrial nations (notably by Italy, Japan and Germany), but it was none the less a favourable result to which devaluation clearly contributed. In dollar terms the export increase was of course less marked, $3\frac{1}{2}$ per cent (again after rough allowance for special influences), because unit values declined by 6 per cent compared with 1967 following the parity adjustment.

The weakness of the trade balance was, therefore, more due to excessive imports, which also rose by 10 per cent in volume. Since the unit value of imports in foreign currency fell by 3 per cent for the year as a whole, the dollar value of imports rose by $6\frac{1}{2}$ per cent and the trade deficit widened. The buoyancy of imports is partly to be explained by special factors: there were large purchases of both diamonds and silver bullion for external account, and the value of fuel imports, inflated as a result of the Middle East war in 1967, remained very high. Of greater fundamental importance, however, was the development of domestic demand and, in particular, of private consumption. Between the third quarter of 1967 and the first three months of 1968 consumer expenditure advanced, at constant prices, at an annual rate of 11 per cent, reflecting earlier reflationary measures as well as anticipation of price increases arising from devaluation and from the March 1968 budget. After a sharp dip in the second quarter of 1968, there was a strong recovery of personal spending after mid-year.

As frequently in the past, this was associated with an excessive increase in wage rates, which, for workers in manufacturing industry, were 9 per cent higher by end-1968 than a year earlier. This outpaced the rise in productivity, and its inflationary impact was all the more severe because of recurrent production stoppages due to an unusual number of industrial disputes. With other domestic demand components moving slowly ahead, the unforeseen buoyancy of consumer expenditure together with the growth of exports caused output to rise strongly, by perhaps as much as 4 per cent in the course of the year, and this was reflected in declining unemployment after the summer. But the strength of total demand also sustained imports, which did no more than flatten out at their high first-quarter level.

Nevertheless, with exports expanding during 1968 while imports were more or less stable, the trade balance did improve in the course of the year. Seasonally adjusted, and after approximate allowance for exports delayed by the 1967 dock strikes, the trade deficit fell from well over $ 0.5 billion in the first quarter to $ 0.3 billion in the fourth.

Even after taking account of the factors mentioned, which acted to keep up the level of imports last year, it was still higher in relation to output than in the past. Whether this is attributed to reversible factors, for example forestalling of possible import restrictions and of a further rise in the final price of imports, or whether to a more lasting influence, such as a shift in the import propensity, has a direct bearing on the size of the further improvement in the trade balance to be expected for 1969. The increase in total demand seems likely to slow down. But this depends largely on consumer spending, at present held back by additional taxation imposed in November, being effectively contained during the rest of the year. This in turn requires tighter control over wages. Public expenditure seems now to be responding to the cuts imposed in January 1968. And the rate of growth of exports may moderate somewhat with an easing of total demand in important markets abroad. Although private investment, in both fixed assets and in stocks, may strengthen, it seems on the whole unlikely that pressure on resources will develop. In this case, and taking account of the import deposit scheme imposed in an already tightening monetary situation, the level of imports might decline on the first interpretation of last year's behaviour or show a renewed moderate rise on the second. Allowing for a programme decline in payments for US military aircraft and for a further increase in net invisible income, a current-account surplus in 1969 of about $ 0.3-0.5 billion might be achieved. While the official target for a surplus at an annual rate of $ 1.2 billion, therefore, still seems out of reach, this would represent a year-to-year improvement of around $ 1½ billion over 1968.

Assuming that there is no serious relapse on long-term capital account —and, with the British Treasury prepared to take over the exchange risk, foreign borrowing by nationalised industries could now give substantial support to the long-term capital balance—progress of this order would do much to restore confidence. Even so, the strength of US demand for liquid funds could inhibit any very large monetary reflow to the United Kingdom, and difficult financing problems associated with scheduled external debt repayments lie ahead. While the short-term outlook, therefore, is not unpromising, it is clear that there is still a long way to go before the United Kingdom's external position is secure. The time when the present elaborate structure of balance-of-payments controls might be dispensed with is not yet in sight.

United States

The US balance-of-payments results for the year 1968 as a whole were very unusual in a number of ways. Firstly, the customary surplus on trade account practically disappeared. Secondly, the United States became a net importer of capital on a rather substantial scale. And thirdly, as the change on the capital account was much bigger even than the deterioration on the foreign trade account, the overall balance of payments went just into surplus (see Table VI).

As measured by the liquidity concept used in the United States, the overall balance improved from a deficit of $ 3.6 billion for 1967 to a small surplus of $ 0.2 billion for 1968. Statistically, this was the best result since the surplus of $ 0.6 billion recorded in 1957. In terms of the official settlements concept—that is, measured simply by the changes in official monetary assets and liabilities—the improvement from 1967 to 1968 was even more striking: from a deficit of $ 3.4 billion to a surplus of $ 1.7 billion. One must seek out the various factors, both real and statistical, which produced these striking changes and try to appraise the underlying position which exists at the present time.

The deterioration in the foreign trade balance between 1967 and 1968 was quite dramatic: from a surplus of $ 3.5 billion to one of slightly less than $ 100 million. It may be noted that exports financed by US foreign aid grants and loans are included in this balance. If they are excluded, then the trade surplus had already disappeared in 1966 and 1967, and there was actually a commercial trade deficit in 1968 of over $ 3 billion.

The deterioration in 1968 occurred despite a rather satisfactory growth of exports over the year, by $ 2.9 billion, or 9 per cent. The export increase, however, was quite overshadowed by an unprecedented rise in imports of $ 6.3 billion, or 23 per cent. Some of this increase, perhaps about 10 per cent, resulted from the strikes in the aluminum and copper industries, together with the threatened strike in the steel industry. But for the most part the upsurge of imports reflected the pressure of excess demand in the US economy.

This pressure was particularly marked during the first half of 1968, when real GNP was rising at an annual rate of 6½ per cent—considerably more than the 4 per cent estimated annual growth of the country's economic potential—and at a rate of 10 per cent in current dollars. The very strong stimulus to expansion during these months came from the public sector of the economy. The net impact of the Federal budget was strongly expansionary, owing to a further sharp acceleration of defence spending. In addition, state and local government expenditures were

Table **VI**

UNITED STATES: BALANCE OF PAYMENTS

		1964
Exports, excluding military (f.o.b.)		25.3
Imports, excluding military (f.o.b.)........................		18.7
Trade balance...		6.6
Investment income	4.7	
Military expenditure	—2.1	
Other	—1.7	
Total services (net)		0.9
Balance on goods and services		7.5
US Government grants and capital (net)..................		—3.6
US private capital (net)		—6.6
Direct investment	—2.3	
Other long-term capital	—2.1	
Short-term capital	—2.2	
Foreign capital (net)		0.7
Errors and omissions		—0.8
Balance on liquidity basis		—2.8
Increase in US liquid liabilities other than to foreign monetary authorities		1.2
Balance on official reserve transactions basis		—1.6

increasing more rapidly than usual. During the second half of the year Federal Government expenditures rose less rapidly; and this, together with the enactment of the 10 per cent tax surcharge, brought the Federal budget into balance by the fourth quarter. At the same time consumers' expenditure rose less than earlier in the year. The rise of real GNP therefore, though still rather high, fell off to an annual rate of about 4½ per cent during the latter part of the year, while in current prices the increase was 8 per cent.

1965		1966		1967		1968	
		in billions of US dollars					
	26.2		29.2		30.5		33.4
	21.5		25.6		27.0		33.3
	4.7		3.6		3.5		0.1
5.1		5.2		5.7		..	
—2.1		—2.9		—3.1		..	
—1.8		—1.8		—2.6		..	
	1.2		0.5		0.0		0.9
	5.9		4.1		3.5		1.0
	—3.4		—3.5		—4.2		—4.1
	—3.8		—4.3		—5.5		—4.8
—3.5		—3.6		—3.0		—3.3	
—1.1		—0.3		—1.3		—1.5	
0.8		—0.4		—1.2			
	0.3		2.5		3.2		8.0
	—0.3		—0.2		—0.6		0.1
	—1.3		—1.4		—3.6		0.2
	0.0		1.7		0.2		1.5
	—1.3		0.3		—3.4		1.7

Other indications of the pressure on resources in 1968 were the larger increases in average hourly earnings from 5 per cent in 1967 to 7 per cent, in wholesale prices from less than 1 per cent to almost 3 per cent, and in consumer prices from just over 3 per cent in 1967 to almost 5 per cent in 1968. At the same time average unemployment fell from 3.8 to 3.5 per cent and to 3.3 per cent by the end of 1968.

Some part of the deterioration in the foreign trade balance during 1968 was offset by an $ 0.9 billion improvement in the services account. Two-thirds of this is accounted for by higher net receipts from investment income and the remainder mainly by a decline in net travel expenditures, which had risen sharply in 1967 owing to the Canadian Exposition. Therefore, the balance on goods and services, on the basis shown in the table, deteriorated by $ 2.5 billion, from $ 3.5 to 1 billion.

Even more striking than the effects of domestic inflation on the trade balance was the reversal of the private capital account, excluding the short-term liabilities of the banks, from a net outflow of $ 2.3 billion in 1967 to a net inflow of $ 3.2 billion. To a considerable extent, this was the result of deliberate action by the US authorities; but, in addition, there was a large increase in foreign purchases of outstanding US securities, mainly common stocks, because of political uncertainties in Europe.

Official policy measures affected the capital account of the balance of payments in three main ways. Firstly, and most important, there was the imposition in January 1968 of mandatory limits on direct investment outflows by US corporations, which were much more severe than the previous voluntary guidelines. This measure did not reduce the total of direct investment, which at $ 3.3 billion was a little higher than in 1967. But it stimulated offshore financing of such investment, as can be seen from the fact that the total of new securities issued abroad by US corporations increased between 1967 and 1968 from under $ 0.5 billion to just over $ 2 billion. And, in addition, it produced large-scale repatriation of investment funds by US corporations in the last weeks of 1968, so as to bring their net direct investment outflows for the year within the ceilings that had been fixed. These repatriations may have amounted to the best part of $ 1 billion and have accounted for most of the sudden improvement in the overall liquidity balance between the third and fourth quarters of 1968, from a surplus of $ 0.1 billion to one of almost $ 1 billion after seasonal adjustment.

Secondly, direct controls on bank lending to non-residents were also tightened in January 1968. Partly as a result of this, and probably also because of the high demand for credit at home, US banks' loans to non-residents, which had risen by $ 460 million in 1967, fell by $ 250 million last year.

Thirdly, there was the continuation, on a larger scale than before, of special official financial transactions between the United States and certain foreign countries. For the most part, these transactions involved shifts of foreign official dollar assets from liquid to non-liquid form; in addition, however, there were in 1968 some special transactions with international organisations, as well as some prepayment of official debt by foreign countries. The total of these special financial transactions (which do not include sales of medium-term Treasury securities denominated in Deutsche Mark to Germany to help offset US military expenditures in that country) amounted to $ 2.3 billion in 1968, as against just under $ 1 billion in 1967.

Altogether the turnround in these three items, most of which is attributable to official US policy measures, must have amounted to $ 4½ billion between 1967 and 1968. On top of this there was a substantial, but quite unrelated, increase of $ 1 billion between the two years in total foreign purchases of outstanding (as opposed to newly issued) US securities—most of which probably represents a flight of capital from Europe induced by political uncertainties.

As already mentioned, the 1968 improvement in the balance of payments, measured on the official settlements basis, was even more striking than on the liquidity basis—from a deficit of $ 3.4 billion to a surplus of $ 1.7 billion. The reason for this was the very large inflow of private funds to the US banking system during the year, mainly from the Euro-dollar market, under the influence of the tight monetary situation in the United States. This inflow, which took the form of a $ 3.8 billion rise in US liquid liabilities to non-official foreigners, counts as a capital inflow in the official settlements balance, whereas in the liquidity balance it is a financing item. Its effect on the official settlements balance was partly offset by the rise of $ 2.3 billion in non-liquid liabilities to foreign official institutions, since this item—which counts as a capital inflow in the liquidity balance—is a monetary item in the official settlements balance. It is because the increase in liquid liabilities to private dollar holders during 1968 exceeded the increase in non-liquid liabilities to official dollar holders by $ 1.5 billion that the official settlements surplus for the year was $ 1.7 billion, as against a liquidity surplus of $ 0.2 billion.

It is clear from these figures that the overall balance-of-payments results for 1968, whether on the liquidity or the official settlements basis, were not only unusual but that they represent the situation in an unduly favourable light. The United States cannot expect a permanent inflow of capital, either from direct controls on investment and official window-dressing operations or from large-scale foreign purchases of US securities or from an inflow to the banks from the Euro-dollar market. Such a pattern would not be appropriate for the richest country in the world and, besides, it is clear that it has been putting the reserve position of other countries under strain. Even if, therefore, some part of the recent changes on private capital account prove to be permanent, the most important balance-of-payments task confronting the United States is to improve the current balance, and more particularly the foreign trade balance, by a very substantial amount. In considering the prospects for this most basic part of the US balance of payments, it is necessary to go back beyond the events of last year.

The decline in the foreign trade surplus in 1968 was exceptionally abrupt, but it followed what had already been a large deterioration during 1965-67. In 1964 there had been a trade surplus of $ 6½ billion—a figure exaggerated by inflationary demand and a poor agricultural season in Europe, which had pushed US exports up by nearly 25 per cent during 1963-64. Then, during 1965-67, excess demand in Europe was brought under better control, leading to a pronounced and widespread cooling off of activity towards the end of this period. At the same time demand pressures in the United States built up steadily as a consequence of the escalating war in Vietnam, and, except for several months of monetary stringency in 1966, US policy did not come to grips with this situation. Mainly as a consequence of these divergent demand developments at home and abroad, US imports in 1967 were already 40 per cent higher than in 1964, while exports had only increased by 20 per cent. By 1967, therefore, the trade surplus had fallen to $ 3½ billion—about equal to the level of US Government financed exports.

It is evident that, if an adequate trade surplus is to be restored, demand inflation in the United States must be arrested. But it is by no means certain that this would be a sufficient remedy. Excess demand in the United States not only damaged the trade balance in the short term but also brought a higher rate of price increase. US export unit values by mid-1968 were 11 per cent higher than in 1964 and this rate of increase was well above that recorded in many other industrial countries. This may have played some part in the fact that the US share in world exports fell from 17.5 per cent in 1964 to 16.3 per cent in the last quarter of 1967. After excess demand has been eliminated, therefore, it may require a period of price stability before the ground lost in international competitiveness can be recovered.

Hence, to return to a trade surplus of the size achieved in 1966 and 1967 may not be easy. And to bring about a situation in which the United States' reserve position stops weakening and in which the variety of direct controls built up in recent years can begin to be dispensed with will require an even more basic adjustment. For that to be possible would, in my view, require that the disequilibrium of the monetary system as a whole be corrected, and not just the US balance of payments alone.

The disequilibrium of the international monetary system

Apart from the imbalances in the payments position of individual countries, which need to be corrected by mutually consistent national adjustment policies, a broader problem affecting the international monetary system as a whole has been evident for some years. It was, in fact, because of this broader problem that the Group of Ten initiated its studies of the functioning of the system in 1963, so as to explore possibilities of correcting the difficulty. As I have recently published an extended analysis of the nature and functioning of the system in the post-war period[1] —which seems to me a self-discipline that anyone proposing reforms of the system should impose on himself—I need here only outline the basic problem and its practical consequences.

The Deputies of the Group of Ten stated in their first report of August 1964 that the flow of new gold available for monetary purposes was not sufficient to provide an adequate growth of global reserves. If that was true in 1964, when official gold stocks increased by more than \$ 700 million, it must be all the more true today, when there is virtually no effective inflow of gold into the monetary system. The question is why and how has the shortage of new gold caused difficulties?

A critical point in the behaviour of the system came in October 1960 when the price of gold in the market rose to over \$ 40 an ounce. Before that time the growth of official reserves in the system came about rather automatically through accumulations of gold and dollars. There was an underlying disequilibrium, however, because the flow of new monetary gold was not large enough to meet central-bank demand, so that the shortage of new supply was made up by a downward trend of US gold reserves. As US liabilities to foreign central banks were steadily rising at the same time as its gold reserves were declining, it eventually became evident that there was a threat to the indefinite convertibility of the dollar at the existing price of gold. It was this danger, which might lead to a rise in the dollar price of gold or to suspension of the convertibility of the dollar, that lay behind the jump in the market price of gold in 1960.

The immediate threat was soon overcome by US assurances that the \$ 35 price would be maintained and by organising the gold pool to

---

1. "The Gold-Dollar System: Conditions of Equilibrium and the Price of Gold", *Essays in International Finance*; October 1968; published by International Finance Section, Princeton University.

manage the market. None the less, the brief interval of gold well above $ 35 left its mark: private demand for gold increased sharply; central-bank preference for gold in the composition of reserves also increased; and, for quite a few central banks, there was reluctance to add to ordinary dollar assets in reserve holdings and there were even efforts to reduce them. Hence, the scope for an autonomous growth of reserves in the system was greatly reduced after 1960, and this produced profound changes in the behaviour of the system.

A possible reaction to these conditions might have been a general tendency to deflation in the world economy. This could have happened if deficit countries had given first priority to maintaining the level of reserves by restrictive fiscal and monetary policies and if other countries adversely affected had likewise sought to defend themselves by restrictive policies. Some commentators during these years believed, in fact, that the absence of general deflation made it evident that there was no shortage of global reserves. But this view overlooked both that the increment to reserves was more important than the global total from an operational standpoint and that the limitation on autonomous reserve growth caused by the shortage of gold was producing quite different responses than general deflation.

What those responses were can be seen from the figures for the period 1961-68 in the table on changes in global reserves. The data are based on IMF statistics, and total reserves are taken to include not only gold and foreign exchange assets but also countries' reserve positions in the IMF. Reserves are reported on a gross basis, that is, without offset for liabilities, which is particularly important for the United States and the United Kingdom in view of their position as reserve currencies (see Table VII).

It can be seen that countries' gold reserves in the aggregate increased by only $ 0.9 billion for the years 1961-68, or at an annual rate of 0.2 per cent. By contrast, the rise from 1951 to 1960 had been $ 4.3 billion, or a rate of 1.2 per cent. One reason for the smaller availability of new monetary gold since 1960 was that ordinary private demand was taking a larger share of new supplies, even though western production increased at a good rate and Russian sales were particularly high in the years 1963-65. The main reason, however, was the large support given to the market from official stocks during the speculative gold-buying wave in late 1967 and the first quarter of 1968.

Table VII

CHANGES IN GLOBAL RESERVES, 1951-68
(in billions of US dollars and average annual percentage increases)

Areas and years	
All countries	
1951-60	
1961-68	
Group of Ten	
1951-60	
1961-68	
Other developed countries	
1951-60	
1961-68	
Less-developed countries	
1951-60	
1961-68	
Group of Ten excluding US and UK	
1951-60	
1961-68	
United States	
1951-60	
1961-68	
United Kingdom	
1951-60	
1961-68	

Despite the smaller contribution of new gold to reserves, it can be seen that global reserves increased by $ 16 billion over the years 1961-68, or at an annual rate of 3.0 per cent. The growth of reserves was actually larger than in the previous decade, when the rate of increase was 2.1 per cent.

Gold		IMF reserve position*	Foreign Exchange		Total	
Amount	%	Amount	Amount	%	Amount	%
+4.3	1.2	+1.9	+ 5.3	3.4	+11.5	2.1
+0.9	0.2	+2.9	+12.2	6.5	+16.0	3.0
+3.9	1.3	+1.6	+ 5.3	9.2	+10.8	2.7
—2.5	.	+2.0	+ 7.7	7.9	+ 7.2	1.8
+0.8	5.6	+0.2	+ 0.0	0.0	+ 1.0	2.2
+2.6	11.8	+0.5	+ 1.7	5.8	+ 4.8	8.9
—0.4	.	+0.1	— 0.0	0.0	— 0.2	.
+0.8	3.2	+0.4	+ 2.9	4.7	+ 4.0	4.5
+9.0	12.6	+1.0	+ 5.5	10.4	+15.4	12.0
+5.7	4.6	+2.8	+ 3.6	4.4	+12.1	5.4
—5.0	.	+0.1	—	—	— 4.9	.
—6.9	.	—0.3	+ 3.5	.	— 3.6	.
—0.1	.	+0.5	— 0.2	.	+ 0.3	0.8
—1.3	.	—0.5	+ 0.5	10.4	— 1.3	.

* Includes gold tranche positions, super gold tranche positions and GAB claims.

It should be noted, however, that in both these periods the rate of growth of global reserves was well below that of world trade. The average annual growth of the latter amounted to 7.4 per cent during 1951-60 and 8 per cent during 1961-68. The ratio of world reserves to world trade turn-over has therefore declined considerably since the beginning of the 1950s and is now rather modest.

To some extent the faster growth of reserves during the period 1961-68 was accounted for by a larger increase in IMF reserve positions—be-cause of increased IMF quotas and drawings by countries on their IMF credit tranches. (Credit tranche drawings produce a rise in total IMF reserve positions because the Fund reserve positions of the drawing countries are, by definition, not affected while those of the lending coun-tries, who are usually in their gold tranches, are increased.) But the bulk of the reserve increase was in foreign exchange holdings, where the rise amounted to $ 12.2 billion, compared with only $ 5.3 billion in 1951-60. While many central banks continued to be quite content to accumulate traditional foreign exchange assets, such as US Treasury bills or time deposits with banks, the essential mechanism which accounts for the rise shown by foreign exchange reserves was special official transactions among the Group of Ten countries. They came about through swap transactions involving dollars and a number of other currencies, through inter-central-bank deposits and through the sale of non-marketable US Treasury securities denominated in foreign currencies. In addition, the sizable portfolio of dollar securities held by the UK Treasury was liquidated and the proceeds transferred to the reserves. In the main these transactions constituted the means used to finance the US and UK external deficits. At the same time they constituted a means of providing acceptable assets to continental European countries that were in external surplus but that did not want either to add unduly to their ordinary dollar exchange holdings or to exert greater pressure on the US gold stock.

These special transactions had the effect of increasing global reserves, of course, because the reserve statistics do not reflect the liabilities of the borrowing countries; in some cases, indeed, such as a wasp of dollars against sterling drawn by the Bank of England on the Federal Reserve, the gross reserves of both countries increase, so that global reserves are increased by double the amount of the swap. It may be estimated that the total statistical effect of special transactions on reserves over these years was more than $ 13 billion, thus exceeding the increase in aggregate foreign exchange holdings. So the possibly deflationary effect of insufficient autonomous reserve growth has been avoided in part by deliberate creation of reserves through official credit transactions negotiated to finance deficits. Another way of putting this is that the growth of global reserves has come to depend on there being payments difficulties somewhere in the system.

Besides liberal use of official credit, the disequilibrium in the system has been met partly by direct controls on exchange transactions. A variety of controls has been set up by the United States and controls have been broadened by the United Kingdom. More recently severe control measures have been instituted by France. On their side, also, several surplus countries have used direct measures to limit excessive inflows of funds from abroad.

Along with the growing reluctance of central banks to accumulate dollar assets unless covered by some sort of exchange guarantee, the shortage of new gold has increased the preference for gold in official reserves. As can be seen in the table on changes in global reserves, this has resulted in an accelerated redistribution of official gold reserves, which had already assumed large proportions in the 1950s. Thus, whereas US gold reserves were reduced by $ 6.9 billion in the period 1961-68 and UK gold holdings fell by $ 1.3 billion, other Group of Ten countries gained $ 5.7 billion of gold and other western world countries $ 3.4 billion. It is evident that this process of redistribution cannot continue very much further without acute danger to the convertibility of the dollar.

To recognise that the shortage of new gold means a disequilibrium for the system as a whole does not, of course, deny that the imbalances in the payments position of a number of countries need to be corrected by more forceful adjustment policies. Both sorts of problems exist and both sorts need to be resolved. However, the existence of the former difficulty imposes a serious obstacle to a solution of the latter. This may be seen by considering the fact that gold is the only means in the present system which allows reserves to increase without a corresponding increase in official liabilities; hence, an inflow of new gold into total reserves provides a margin for countries to have a surplus balance-of-payments position without other countries having deficits. When there is no inflow of new gold into the system, however, this margin does not exist and the improvement of deficits requires that other countries' positions deteriorate. This is bound to be resisted before the process of adjustment goes very far, since it is impossible to expect that the deterioration will hit only surplus countries with sufficiently large reserves which they do not mind seeing decline.

At the present time, in fact, we are seeing such a pressure on reserves. As already discussed above, the United States had a surplus on an official settlements basis in 1968, due essentially to very large capital imports and to the inflow of money to the banks from the Euro-dollar market. With monetary restraint even tighter in the first months of 1969, US banks have continued to bid strongly for Euro-dollars, with the consequence that there has been a series of defensive discount rate changes by other central banks.

Faced with the present dilemma of the system, some commentators believe the way out to be a realignment of exchange rates in order to adjust persistent deficit and surplus positions in one multilateral operation. Without passing judgment on the desirability or practicality of such an operation, one can say that it would be logical if it included an adjustment of the price of gold. However, the same commentators seem to believe that there is something mysteriously sacred about the price of gold which puts it outside the category of exchange rates. In reality, of course, the dollar price of gold is the exchange rate of the dollar, and the price of gold in all currencies is the exchange rate between all currencies and gold.

It seems to me, therefore, that the problem of gold is the key question with regard to the future of the monetary system. If gold is to perform its normal role in the system, action must be taken to assure an adequate regular inflow of gold to monetary reserves. If not, the monetary authorities must reach a workable arrangement for the full management of gold in the composition of reserves, probably with the implication that gold must be a generally inactive reserve asset. In the meantime, one can expect a continual menace of crisis, resort to direct exchange controls, financing by special transactions, difficulties in maintaining fixed rates and a growing proportion of illiquid assets in reserves.

Chapter III

MULTILATERAL SURVEILLANCE, CONSULTATION, AND THE ADJUSTMENT PROCESS

by *Robert W. Russell*

When discussing changes which may occur in the international monetary system during coming years, the opportunity for realizing permanent improvement through programmed reform ought not to obscure the presence of a number of fundamental difficulties in international monetary relations which cannot be fully eliminated but could be somewhat reduced. The problem of maintaining or restoring equilibrium in the external payments of nations is one such difficulty. Alternative structures for the international monetary system change the frequency and degree to which disequilibria in payments (in the form of surpluses and deficits on a liquidity basis) emerge, and the seriousness with which they are treated. But as long as nations retain the ability to take independent economic decisions, those decisions will have an effect upon international monetary relations which will require nations to take measures of adjustment, that is, measures to establish a new level of equilibrium in their international payments. The assumption here is that the problem of adjustment in international payments is a permanent one, although it is influenced by the structure of the international monetary system, and that arrangements for coping with the adjustment problem ought to take cognizance of its ultimate insolubility.

Within that context there are a number of relevant lessons to be drawn from the recent history of monetary relations among the major non-socialist industrialized nations. That history is especially instructive because the current structure of the international monetary system places significantly higher demands on the process of balance of payments adjustment than do other historical and theoretical structures. As a response to this stress on the adjustment process, a variety of arrangements for international consultation have evolved which have as their central purpose the preservation of balance of payments equilibrium through stimulation of appropriate adjustment policies by member nations. By examining the impact of these consultative arrangements upon the adjustment policies of the participants some hypotheses can be made about the likelihood that equilibrium can be guaranteed through international discussions, and the consequences of that probability for the desirability of changing the structure of the international monetary system.

Structural variables and the "need" for adjustment

At least five discernible variables located in the structure of the international monetary system condition both the presence of disequilibria in national payments and the perceived need for removing such disequilibria. Stated simple they are:
1. freedom for international economic transactions;
2. alterability of exchange rates;
3. amount, growth and distribution of internationally acceptable monetary reserves;
4. autonomous mechanisms for adjustment;
5. external holding of national currencies.

These variables are described below with respect to their effect upon the adjustment process in the current period, but with consideration for effects which might be expected under other conditions than those presently prevailing in the international monetary system.

Maximizing freedom for international economic transactions is a stated goal of a number of organizations, among which the International Monetary Fund, the General Agreement on Tariffs and Trade, and the Organization for Economic Cooperation and Development deserve special mention because of the breadth of their membership and the priority which they attach to that objective. Generally the non-socialist industrialized nations favor the maximum freedom for economic transactions in the belief that maximum efficiency in the use of the world's resources is thereby assured and consequently that maximum wealth for all nations is thereby achieved. Logically the maximalization principle would include free movement for factors of production besides goods and services, but most nations have been reluctant to permit the labor factor (people) to move freely and hesitant or uncertain about flows of capital investment. Nevertheless the present era is noteworthy for the amount of freedom which is granted to the international exchange of both products and factors of economic production. As a consequence of the considerable freedom for transactions there is less certainty that the balance of payments of individual nations will be in equilibrium. The contrast with a state trading system illustrates an alternative situation in which equilibrium is precisely guaranteed, but freedom is absent. From the standpoint of economic efficiency, the preference for maximum freedom for transactions is unassailable, but the more freely transactions occur, the more probable is the appearance of balance of payments disequilibria (at least in the range short of total freedom for all forms of exchange or the adoption of a common monetary policy, either of which would negate the nation itself as an entity).

The rates at which national currencies are exchanged have an inverse relationship to freedom and adjustment. If rates were permitted to fluctuate with absolute freedom from interference by national authorities, there would be no problem of adjustment. Disequilibria in payments would be transmitted into changes in exchange rates. There is no necessity to raise questions here about the effect of freely fluctuating rates upon investment and trade, since a condition in which no trade occurred would be one of perfect adjustment at zero equilibrium in the balance of payments of each country. The significant point is that flexibility in exchange rates can absorb some of the need for adjustment, and that the more fixed the rates of exchange, the more serious will be the need for adjustment. The present IMF Articles of Agreement provide that exchange rates may vary no more than 1% above or below their stated gold parity. Alterations in parities are permitted only in cases of "fundamental disequilibrium". Widening of the margins of permissible variation (the band) would require a formal decision by the Fund. This adjustable peg system has become further rigidified since the introduction in 1958 of general convertibility for Western European currencies. Since the revaluation of the German mark and Dutch guilder in 1961, the tendency has been for nations to resist either revaluations or devaluations for as long as possible. The "pegged" portion of the system has been emphasized, with the result that increased pressure is placed upon nations to operate their economies in a way that will assure equilibrium in each nation's balance of payments.

A factor particularly salient for individual nations is the relationship between the availability of internationally acceptable monetary reserves and the need for adjustment of a payments disequilibrium. Avoiding for the moment the special case of key currencies (that is, assuming that disequilibria in the liquidity balance are quickly and uniformly translated into reserve flows), a useful distinction can be made between the attitudes of surplus and deficit countries toward changes in holdings of reserves. The assumption is sometimes made that surplus countries are willing to accumulate reserves infinitely. While that is a useful approximation of reality, it ignores the nature of reserves and the interdependency of the modern international system. Whether the reserve accumulation comes in the form of a national or an international currency, the surplus country may began to lose confidence in the value of that currency as a monetary reserve for the future. If that circumstance is accompanied by the fear that to refuse to allow the deficit nations to finance their deficits in this way could lead to a collapse of the entire trading system and a world economic depression, the surplus nation is caught in a nasty dilemma. To protect the system from disaster and perhaps to protect the value of the reserves it has already accumulated, the surplus nation may feel itself compelled to pursue an expansionary domestic policy or revalue its currency or make generous loans to the deficit nation. Therefore, it is not always the case that surplus nations are willing to see disequilibria persist.

The common assumption with respect to deficit countries is that they cannot permit their reserves to decline infinitely since they possess only a finite amount of such reserves. That assumption neglects the possibility for infinite borrowing of reserves. A nation may be less inclined to remove its deficit position if it can always count upon other nations to provide credit to cover the deficits. In this case the deficit country may be able to pressure the surplus country into performing the primary task of adjustment, although in general deficit countries feel more compulsion to adjust their economies to remove the deficit condition.

An additional general characteristic of national behaviour with respect to monetary reserves is that most nations prefer to see the absolute amount of their reserves increase over time, that is, most nations wish to be in a long term surplus condition. That desire can only be met when the total quantity of world reserves increases over time in an amount sufficient to meet that need. If the level of reserves remains static or declines, the struggle between the nations may be so severe that the entire system collapses. From the viewpoint of facilitating the adjustment process, the total quantity of international reserves ought to increase, but the amount of reserve growth ought not to be so great as to sanctify the perpetual operation by certain nations in a deficit position. Large increases in international reserves may reduce the attractiveness of those reserves for the surplus nations, and place those nations in a weaker position when the burden of adjusting is distributed.

The fourth major structural factor in the international monetary system which conditions the need for adjustment is the presence of autonomous adjusting mechanisms. Payments surpluses and deficits produce direct effects upon domestic incomes and liquidity which tend to restore an equilibrium level of international payments. An indirect monetary effect is also operative. Two major difficulties exist which prevent these automatic mechanisms from solving the adjustment problem. First, national authorities often do not permit the income and liquidity effects to operate, preferring to neutralize and counteract those effects because they interfere with the achievement of other national objectives. Second, a country may experience major shifts in productivity, investment or other factors which are not reversible, or are not sufficiently compensated for by the automatic mechanisms. It is probably true to say that in theory the automatic adjustment mechanisms could have been more influential in restoring international payments equilibria in recent years, but that they will never handle all cases of disequilibrium in an appropriate manner.

There is a final factor which has been especially troublesome in the most recent period of international monetary relations: the special status of so-called key currencies. The currencies of certain nations (the dollar and pound sterling in recent years) are sometimes accumulated by other nations as official monetary reserves and by private firms as transactions currencies. The nation whose currency is in demand for these purposes can run a deficit in its balance of payments for an indefinite period without losing its own monetary reserves. But unless these external accumulations of national currency are the product of agreed, guaranteed arrangements, there is a nagging uncertainty about the permanence of the "holding" action. That has been the situation of the United States dollar for several years, and explains the ambivalence the Americans have shown about removing their deficits as well as the ambivalence of other countries about desiring the elimination of those deficits as a source of dollars. To the extent that national currencies are held abroad, the adjustment of payments imbalances will not be viewed as desirable by either surplus or deficit nations. A major source of difficulty for the system is the failure of surplus and deficit nations to agree upon the amounts of national currencies to be permanently held. The adjustment process is encumbered by the lack of agreement upon how much imbalance ought to be tolerated.

From even a brief sketch of the relationship between the principal structural variables in the international monetary system and the need for adjustment, the heavy pressure placed upon the adjustment process at present seems obvious. Considerable freedom for economic transactions, resistance to changes in exchange rates, the slow growth of acceptable monetary reserves, the neglect or failure of automatic mechanisms for adjustment and the disputes over permissible foreign accumulations of dollars and sterling—all these together—constitute the structure of the international monetary system today and that structure is designed (perhaps unintentionally) to place maximum stress upon the willingness of nations to keep their economies closely in line with price and cost trends in other major nations. Policy measures must be adopted to keep national economic indicators in line with fixed rates of exchange, but these policy measures are sovereign national decisions over which no international organization has any supra-national authority. From the viewpoint of the national decisionmakers, the appropriate policy from an international adjustment perspective may conflict with other domestic economic objectives concerning employment, national growth, price stability etc., not to mention the goals of national foreign policy. Furthermore, the fact that adjustment measures can be taken by either surplus or deficit countries or both in a variety of combinations encourages each country to place the responsibility upon other nations whenever convenient to do so. In an attempt to satisfy the international need for adjustment, nations have created a number of international bodies where *de facto* negotiations can occur about which nations ought to take measures to restore balance in international payments.

The growth of international monetary consultations

Only a broad survey can be made here of the international organizations actively engaged in securing better balance of payments adjustment policies among the principal industrial countries. Clearly the International Monetary Fund has special responsibilities in this area, but for a variety of reasons the Fund has not been the principal actor. The Fund has devoted much of its attention to the payments problems of the developing countries and has assisted them in adopting sounder economic policies. The sheer size of the Fund membership makes it difficult for effective consultation to be conducted among the member nations, and for the Fund to devote adequate attention to every monetary problem. There is an additional restraint upon the Fund in its practice of engaging in pervasive inspection of a country's payments situation only when that country makes drawings from its credit tranches in the Fund. Despite the recent emergence of annual visits by the Fund Staff to all nations, the impression is that the Fund must focus its efforts upon deficit nations and can not give continuous attention to the adjustment process in all major countries.[1]

A number of financial arrangements which have been erected alongside the Fund are more directly interesting for a study of international consultations upon adjustment policy. The impetus for these new arrangements stemmed from the great increase in European dollar balances caused by the large American deficits from 1958 to 1960. The Kennedy administration was forced to give serious attention to this problem, and the President's balance of payments program announced February 6, 1961 promised to reduce the American deficit sharply. Through a number of initiatives by the United States Treasury and Federal Reserve System, substantial secondary lines of defense for the dollar were devised and European confidence partially restored in the immutability of the dollars' gold price. Since most of these institutions and agreements still influence the adjustment process, a few facts concerning the membership and functions of these entities might be recalled.

An extraordinarily large sum of money for the time ($ 6 billion) was involved in the conclusion of the General Agreements to Borrow in Paris, December 1961, between the International Monetary Fund and ten major industrial nations.[2]

The parties to the agreements promise to make specified amounts of their currencies available to the Fund in cases of serious danger to the international monetary system. No country is under obligation to provide funds unless it agrees with the Fund as to the seriousness of the situation. This Group of Ten (now eleven) has not developed into a cabinet for the Fund or a new governing board.

Perhaps the best description is that the Group of Ten is an occasional

---

1. A more thorough analysis of the Fund's role would be valuable, but was not possible within the time allotted to the present research.
2. They are: Belgium, Canada, France, Italy, Japan, The Netherlands, Sweden, West Germany, United Kingdom and United States. Switzerland became associated with the group in 1964.

caucus of very important powers. The Ministers of Treasury and central bank Governors of the eleven countries meet an average of twice per year. Except for sessions which occur as adjuncts to Fund Annual Meetings, these Group of Ten meetings are arranged *ad hoc* when the situation warrants and in a location of convenience. The Ten have no staff, no budget, no office, nor is there any apparent need for formalization. Mention should also be made of the existence of the Group of Ten Deputies in addition to the Group of Ten itself.

The Deputies consist of the principal subordinates to the Ministers and Governors of the eleven countries, and these Deputies have met frequently in connection with special studies ordered by the Group of Ten and during the drafting of the Special Drawing Rights proposal. The Deputies have sometimes borrowed staff temporarily from other organizations. Together, the Group of Ten and the Deputies of the Ten have been responsible for making fundamental decisions about the structure and course of international monetary relations, despite the irregularity with which they have met.

The United States took a further precautionary step by encouraging the emergence and expansion of "swap" agreements between the Federal Reserve System and foreign central banks on a bilateral basis. The agreements provide simply for short-term exchanges of national currencies between two banks. With the addition of swap agreements between various European central banks, an entire network of swap arrangements has come into existence since 1961.[3] Other monetary innovations introduced in the early 1960's include Roosa bonds (United States treasury bonds denominated for payment in the currency of the purchasing country), non-negotiable instruments bearing gold guarantees, and American interventions in forward exchange markets through accumulation and disposal of foreign currencies. The most bothersome effect of these measures was to obscure the actual balance of payments situation in the United States and other major countries, even from the central

---

3. See the accounts in the March and September issues of the *Federal Reserve Bulletin* since 1962.

bankers and government officials who inaugurated the activities. The need for a more thorough and frequent interchange of financial statistics among the major industrialized nations was dramatized.

Simultaneously with the new seriousness attached to the United States balance of payments program, the formation of the Group of Ten and other measures, the Organization for European Economic Cooperation was undergoing a metamorphosis into the Organization for Economic Cooperation and Development. The OEEC had been concerned with the coordination of the economic policies of the European recipients of Marshall Plan aid. The new OECD hoped to perform an analogous economic coordination task for its enlarged membership including the United States, Canada and Japan. Besides its central concern for economic growth in the developed member nations, the OECD intended to take on new responsibilities, in the coordination of aid to developing nations and in the easing of the balance of payments situation which appeared especially threatening in 1961. At the initiative of the United States delegation a subcommittee of the Economic Policy Committee known as Working Party 3 was formed in April 1961 to discuss problems related to the balance of payments.[4]

The Working Party is composed of representatives of the same countries as the Group of Ten.[5]

One of the indications of the success and importance of the meetings is that they have been attended by high-ranking officials consistently since 1961. Ordinarily three or four persons per country attend, with at least one person from the central bank and one from the government finance ministry. Those countries with special governmental offices for internal economic policy customarily include a top official from that agency in their delegation. Quite often members of the Group of Ten Deputies Central Bank representatives who meet regularly at Basle, and members of the various committees of the European Communities are

---

4. A good account from the American side is: Robert V. Roosa, *The Dollar and World Liquidity* (New York: Random House, 1967, pp. 25-32).
5. Belgium, though not an official member, has achieved a form of participation in the meetings.

reunited at the meetings of Working Party 3. This overlap of attendance and membership permits a more personal relationship among those present and encourages an exchange of views which is both more friendly and more honest than is sometimes the case in international organizations.

Meetings are held at six to eight week intervals and Working Party 3 has its own staff within the OECD Secretariat who prepare confidential statistical reports, special study papers and twice yearly composite balance of payments figures. These figures include projections into future time periods as well as current and past performance records. The projections are intended to assist in a traditional purpose of the meetings: to reconcile the balance of payments aims of the member states. In the beginning, national representatives appearing at Working Party 3 often presented prepared statements based on national statistics designed to minimize the importance of recent movements in their payments. After considerable effort the Secretariat devised a presentation for balance of payments statistics which rendered national figures compatible. On the basis of these common statistics the discussions became less formal and more frank over the years.

Although the remainder of this paper is focused upon Working Party 3, there are three additional international organizations which have a direct concern with balance of payments adjustments policies; EEC, BIS and GATT. The European Economic Community has formed a number of Committees to assist in integrating the adjustment policies of its Six members. The oldest and most influential of these is the Monetary Committee composed of representatives of the finance ministries who meet about every three weeks. Others are the Committee of Central Bank Governors, the Short Term Policy Committee and Budgetary Policy Committee. The EEC has made important contributions to the reconciliation of conflicting national economic policy objectives and its experience may contain lessons for groups with larger, more diverse membership. Nor should the Bank for International Settlements at Basle be overlooked. The BIS was nearer to the center of monetary policy during the days of the European Payments Union, but continues to provide important services to many European nations. Because of its long history in confidential handling of financial information, the BIS has acquired new functions in recent years as major nations have intensified their contacts and exchanges of such information. The General Agreement on Tariffs and Trade has the responsibility for encouraging the progressive removal of barriers to international trade and judging whether national policies which are ostensibly aimed at restoring balance in international payments are consistent with the rules of GATT. This involves the GATT in deciding which measures may properly be used to remove deficit and surplus positions and under what circumstances they may be used. The GATT, BIS, EEC, the Fund, OECD and the Group of Ten have all been engaged in international consultations of increasing intensity directed toward solution of balance of payments adjustment problems.

The search for rules for adjustment policy

Besides the proliferation of consultative organs, the concern for improved adjustment policies led the major nations to seek new ways to organize their consultations and to attempt to formulate commonly agreed rules to govern national economic behaviour to insure the maintenance or restoration of equilibrium payments conditions. One fundamental reform which attracted major attention and general interest was the search for a new source of international monetary reserves to be created by internationally agreed procedures and in agreed amounts. The second concern was related to the persistent deficits of the United States and the United Kingdom and aimed at strengthening the consultative process in ways that would place more pressure upon nations in payments imbalance to correct their positions.

At the Annual Meeting of the Fund in Washington, D.C. on October 2, 1963, it was announced that the Group of Ten through its Deputies would undertake a study of the "outlook for the functioning of the international monetary system and of its future needs for liquidity." The United States, acting upon an initiative by the United Kingdom, was instrumental in arranging for this study within the Group of Ten Deputies. The Deputies' meetings revealed that the interest in some form of additional international liquidity was countered by a concern that the major deficit nations were not fully disclosing the seriousness of their difficulties and might use any additional liquidity to avoid necessary adjustment measures. Both objectives were accommodated in the Deputies' Report to the Group of Ten at their Paris meeting, June, 1964.

The Deputies concluded that the supply of international liquidity might indeed prove to be inadequate in the future, and recommended a further study of possible remedies through creation of a new reserve asset. That study was conducted by a group of experts chaired by the Hon. Rinaldo Ossola of the Bank of Italy, and the results published in August, 1965 as the *Report of the Study Group on the Creation of Reserve Assets* (Rome: Bank of Italy Press, 1965). The report was followed by a series of negotiations in the Fund, the EEC Monetary Committee and the Group of Ten which resulted in the succesful formulation of the plan for Special Drawing Rights in the Fund. Those negotiations form a most interesting historical episode in international monetary relations, but cannot be included in the present account.

The Deputies were equally interested in the question of adjustment and perceived an obligation for nations to engage in international consultation "to ensure so far as possible that adjustment measures adopted by national authorities take adequate account of the interests of other countries". The report proposed a system of "multilateral surveillance of bilateral financing and liquidity creation" to be implemented through provision of technical information to BIS followed by a "full exchange of views" in Working Party 3. This would provide a basis for "multilateral surveillance of the various elements of liquidity creation, with a view to avoiding excesses or shortages in the means of financing existing or anticipated surpluses and deficits in the balance of payments, and to *discussing measures appropriate for each country* in accordance with the general economic outlook."[6]

---

6. Paragraphs 8, 35-37 of the Annex Prepared by Deputies to the Ministerial Statement of the Group of Ten issued August 10, 1964. Emphasis added.

The Deputies recommended that in addition to the system of multi-lateral surveillance there be a further study by Working Party 3 of the measures and instruments "which are best adapted to avoiding imbalance and to correcting it as early and as smoothly as possible when it occurs." This study would "explore whether *standards* could be formulated on the contribution of monetary and related policies to balance of payments equilibrium, *against which the performance of countries could be appraised.*"[7] The intention of some members of the Group of Ten Deputies in assigning to the Working Party the task of studying the adjustment process was that the report would include clearly defined "rules of the game" which surplus and deficit countries should observe, almost a codification of international monetary theory. Once the rules had been defined, the Working Party with the assistance of multilateral surveillance function could perform a quasi-adjudicative role in determining whether nations were observing these standards.

The Ministers and Governors of the Group of Ten accepted the Deputies' recommendations, thus launching both multilateral surveillance and the special Working Party 3 study of the adjustment process. They affirmed the importance of adjustment in their statement:

"The smooth functioning of the international monetary system depends on the avoidance of major and persistent imbalances and on the effective use of appropriate policies by national governments to correct them when they occur."[8]

A report on the adjustment process was published by Working Party 3 in August, 1966, but that report does not fulfill the implicit expectation present in the mandate to the Working Party that it would draw up a list of rules of economic behavior to complement the informational exchange occurring through multilateral surveillance. A distinction is made in the report between the actions which might be required to prevent the emergence of disequilibria and those which would be required to correct disequilibria which were already present in the system. The value of

---

7. *Ibid.*, paragraphs 9-10, emphasis added.
8. Ministerial Statement, paragraph 3.

multilateral surveillance as an informational exchange is emphasized by the suggestion that an "early warning system" be devised, based upon statistical indicators. Presumably a close analysis of data would assist policymakers in predicting the emergence of disequilibria, and in deciding what rules were applicable for the prevention of that situation. But the report concluded that rules for preventive action cannot be formulated and that only a few broad rules of prudence dare be indicated:

"It is the majority view . . . (that because of) the wide differences between countries in traditions, institutions, ecomonic and financial structure, and government practices and also because of the different requirements and possibilities for policy mix in different situations, *it is not possible to establish quantitative relationships* between certain economic variables which would be appropriate to all countries in all circumstances."[9]

If not preventive rules, then perhaps the Working Party could devise rules to correct existing disequilibria. But after reviewing three possibilities for policy guidelines, the report concluded that they:

"provide a set of presumptions concerning the appropriate broad types of measure which should at least form a useful framework within wich adjustment policies can, in individual cases, be discussed and evaluated. But *they can be regarded as no more than a highly-simplified framework, since*, as recent experience shows, *imbalances are frequently of a far more complex nature*. This has, for example, been clearly apparent from the Working Party's discussions in recent years concerning the United States, the United Kingdom, Germany and Italy."[10]

By rejecting the possibility that any policy guidelines could be established for the major deficit nations—the United States and the United Kingdom—the Working Party report effectively denied the existence of rules for adjustment behavior either to correct or prevent imbalances in international payments. The majority of the member nations preferred not to construct a normative guide to national behavior, but to substitute a proposal for an early warning system and to encourage the Working Party to:

"continue and strengthen its *confrontation of national policies*, with a view to the critical evaluation both of their appropriateness from the point of view of the country concerned, and of their impact on other countries."[11]

The influence of surveillance and consultation

Working Party 3 presently performs four functions in relation to the adjustment process. First, it shares with BIS the conduct of multilateral surveillance over the means by which nations finance their surpluses and deficits, which responsibility can be broadly defined as one of informational exchange. Second, the Working Party is supposed to warn nations that are presently in equilibrium about dangerous tendencies in their payments and to convince those nations to take appropriate measures to halt these tendencies, essentially a preventive function. Third, the Working Party, along with the Fund, the EEC and other organizations, promotes restoration of balance of payments equilibrium by advising nations as to appropriate corrective policy measures. Finally, together with GATT and the Fund, Working Party 3 shapes the atmosphere of the international monetary system to tolerate or discourage the pursuit of balance of payments policies which interfere with the principle of maximalization of freedom for economic transactions. This latter function is not specifically acknowledged by OECD, but it clearly is operational in practice.

Multilateral surveillance was inaugurated in 1964 when the members of the Group of Ten began providing monthly confidential statistical information on their latest, external monetary position to the Bank for International Settlements in Basle. Since most European central banks

---

11. *Adjustment Process*, paragraph 71.

already participated in the BIS and were accustomed to meeting monthly to discuss the latest international currency flows, all that was new was United States participation and a more extensive exchange of information than had been the previous practice. That information includes accounts of swap transactions, a particular source of concern when the system was proposed. Reports vary as to whether nations indicate their exact involvement in forward exchange markets, but there is consensus that the information is generally complete and up-to-date.

The exchanges of statistical information are monthly events, but the multilateral surveillance exercise and the informal conversations of the central bank Governors occur every two months at Basle in an atmosphere of strict secrecy. The danger that information leaks could encourage private speculation in the exchange markets is treated seriously. BIS has the responsibility for providing statistical information to Working Party 3 for multilateral surveillance, and the central bank Governors must decide whether to temporarily withhold certain items of information. This necessity has not proven troublesome to the deliberations in Working Party 3.

Multilateral surveillance at BIS includes discussions about the appropriateness of various methods of financing surplus and deficit positions and national monetary policies. These conversations are not so extensive as those at Working Party 3, and it should be recalled that central banks do not customarily have broad control over adjustment measures. Many important policy decisions concerning adjustment are made by governments, and governments are not represented at Basle. Bearing that precaution in mind, it may still be assumed that the conversations at BIS have an important impact on short-term measures such as swaps, exchange market interventions, discount rates, and assorted special financing arrangements. Generally the talks at Basle are more technical, confidential and expert than those at Paris. Working Party 3 must consider political problems which seldom intrude upon the monetary meetings at BIS.

The role of Working Party 3 in the exchange of information is largely passive. Meetings of Working Party 3 at OECD are based upon a formal agenda and a collection of statistics and papers. The information provided by BIS to the working Party is supplemented by an oral non-quantified presentation which serves to indicate the trends in figures not immediately reported. The most important contribution of Working Party 3 is that countries use the meeting as an outlet to explain major policy steps upon which they have already decided. The country making such announcements often hopes to mobilize support or at least acceptance for the decision it has taken. The listeners can learn the intentions of a country as well as the reasons for a policy move. The country reveals its attitudes toward its own policy. Because these policy explanations occur regularly in a close, confidential atmosphere they help to allay mutual suspicion and to avoid recrimination. This may explain why the international monetary system has weathered several monetary crises and the imposition of various controls on economic transactions without triggering a chain reaction of beggar-thy-neighbor measures.

The preventive function has proven far more difficult to implement because of the failure to devise an effective early warning system either in Working Party 3 or elsewhere (some reports say that the Monetary Committee of the European Community has more success in predicting balance of payments trends for its five major economic units). Working Party 3 does include regular balance of payments forecasts in its statistical reports, and has even included "alternative forecasts" to account for certain possible developments. There has been no attempt to devise alternative forecasts on the basis of hypothetical policy choices for individual nations. Giving warning in terms of specific policies might come too close to sovereign national powers to be tolerable. A certain kind of preventive function has been played by Working Party 3 through exposing the members to a common assessment of their national economic objectives for future periods. Promoting consistency of balance of payments aims has been a purpose of the group since 1961. There are indications that the exchange of views in the Working Party has discouraged the assumption of extreme stances, and, while not guaranteeing the consistency of aims, has enhanced the recognition of inconsistencies.

To accomplish its third function, promotion of proper corrective adjustment policies, Working Party 3, must depend primarily upon the active trading of criticism and comment in the meetings. The discussions are not usually aimed at specific policy suggestions, but more toward indicating to a country where the dangers lie and in which direction it ought to be working. This criticism has the important role of letting a country whether the other nations believe its explanation of its situation. The comments may bring to a country's attention an aspect it has neglected and may even lead to a reconsideration and re-evaluation of policy. Certainly the discussion will strengthen those within a government who wish to take an internationally responsible, but internally unpopular decision. To supplement these discussions the international personality of Working Party 3 has developed formal as well as informal procedures for making its collective opinion known to officials of nations with distinct payments disequilibria. This communication of collective judgment is conveyed to countries in surplus position as well as those in deficit, but results have been more observable in the latter group. There are also considerable national variations in the extent to which influence is successfully exercised. The United States and the United Kingdom have both at times felt relatively impervious to international criticism by reason of their critical position in the support of the general system. The continental surplus countries have at times felt rather smug about their growing reserves and indifferent to suggestions that they take adjustment measures. Fortunately such attitudes have not been typical of the process as a whole. However, they do serve as a reminder that adjustment measures depend upon the political willingness of sovereign nations to take them.

Working Party 3 has also had a significant role in the largely negative function of policing exceptions to the free movement of products, factors and payments. Within this area the granting and withholding of toleration by members of Working Party 3 has made possible the concrete shaping of adjustment programs, despite the absence of any formal sanctioning authority. The ideology of OECD and Working Party 3 has always favored maximum freedom for international economic transactions. Member nations are expected to employ monetary and fiscal instruments to achieve payments adjustments before resorting to inhibitions and controls upon the movement of trade and capital. When a country does find it necessary to adopt restrictive measures, Working Party 3 insists that the restrictions be temporary and be removed as soon as the payments situation eases. Since restrictions have been permitted on several recent occasions and have brought criticism of the international monetary system, this subject demands elaboration.

Working Party 3 has a clear discrepancy in its attitude toward trade restrictions and capital restrictions. Quantitative controls on trade are strictly prohibited, and a measure such as the British import surtax is only accepted after serious confrontations of opinion. Direct, pointed pressure is applied to have these trade measures removed quickly, as was done in the British case. Capital, particularly short-term varieties, is treated differently. Because capital movements occur more rapidly than adjustment measures take effect, controls are often thought to be necessary to give adjustment time to happen. After initial hesitation, the members have concluded that destabilizing capital movements cannot always be controlled by interest rates and exchange market interventions. While the desire to return to freer capital markets persists, there is little pressure in that direction. In the case of the United States capital controls, preference for retention has been expressed.

In each of the four functions just discussed, Working Party 3 must depend upon the cooperation of sovereign nations in order to have any success in improving the chances for equilibrium in international payments. The level of that cooperation is probably not dependent upon the forum provided by Working Party 3, although the usefulness of that forum is not denied. It is not possible to say how nations would have behaved in the absence of these consultative procedures, but the impression of many of those who have participated in multilateral surveillance and in the confrontations in Working Party 3 is that the meetings have had only a modest influence upon the policy decisions of member countries. That influence has been greatest when advice was given to a deficit country anticipating the need for obtaining international credits from the same nations whose representatives comprise Working Party 3. Surplus nations have been less attentive because they have less expectation of requiring assistance. Through multilateral surveillance of the way a nation finances its deficits, it has been possible to compel a nation to dip more deeply into its reserves than it would have preferred, or to make a drawing upon the Fund, instead of relying upon swap transactions. Beyond the *de facto* linkage between consultations in Working Party 3 and the provision of additional monetary reserves to deficit nations, there is little discernible evidence that the consultative procedures exert a direct influence upon the adjustment policy decisions of the major industrialized countries. Undoubtedly these discussions facilitate international economic cooperation when nations are already disposed to cooperate, but the fiber of surveillance and consultation is not strong enough to guarantee that nations will take concerted measures to correct payments disequilibria.

International adjustment in the future

The conclusion emerging from a review of the consultative machinery available to reconcile the conflicting economic policies of the major nations must certainly be that that machinery is hardly adequate to meet the task of international balance of payments adjustment, as long as the need for adjustment is so directly concentrated upon these arrangements. The only reasonable recommendations for improvement within the present structure are more in the nature of tinkering than fundamental alteration. Perhaps the secretariats of the various international organizations could prepare more provocative research studies; perhaps more publication of the findings of the international meetings would compel governments to act more readily; perhaps governments could place more authority for adjustment policy measures in the hands of national officials who attend these meetings. Such steps would certainly enhance the probability of arriving at mutually compatible conclusions and policy measures, but would they be sufficient without reforming the structure of the international monetary system?

The five variables mentioned earlier in this paper could be changed in a way to reduce the need for international balance of payments adjustment. Economic transactions could be controlled, exchange rates could be made more flexible, an adequate, but not excessive growth of reserves could be arranged, freer play could be given to the automatic adjustment effects of payments, and the holding of national currencies in foreign currencies could be regulated. Within this group of possibilities there are clear differences in the economic desirability and political feasibility of their adoption. The free flow of economic transactions should not be disrupted until the alternatives have been tried, otherwise the efficient use of economic resources is reduced. Paradoxically, much of the effort to date to restore balance of payments equilibrium has resulted in exactly the kind of restrictions that ought to be avoided. Would it not be better to launch modest experiments with the alternatives?

The most fundamental and promising structural changes would be to make exchange rates somewhat more flexible than at present and to activate the SDR arrangement for managed growth in world monetary reserves. Flexibility in rates could be accomplished in a variety of ways, but whatever scheme is decided upon ought not to unduly hamper the flow of international trade and investment or stimulate speculation. To meet these conditions, flexibility must be limited in scope and either very gradual or unpredictable in occurrence, which might suggest that so little flexibility would be achieved that no great advantage in adjustment would result. However, even a small dose of flexibility would absorb some of the need for payments adjustment, and correspondingly reduce the need for deliberate adjustment measures.

None of the possible changes in the international monetary system would completely remove the need for nations to take adjustment measures, that is, to make national economic policy decisions with awareness of the payments effects upon foreign countries. Some changes could reduce the need to adjust payments through measures agreed upon in international consultations. Confrontations between sovereign nations cannot be expected to result in perfect economic policy coordination, no matter how skillfully the meetings are conducted. Proposals to reform the monetary system should recognize the need to reduce the magnitude of the adjustment task assigned to such consultations, while remembering the necessity for preserving those procedures to deal with the lingering problem of integrating national economic policy with the international system.

Chapter IV

THE FUTURE OF THE INTERNATIONAL RESERVE ASSETS

by *Edward M. Bernstein*

Summary

The holding of gold, dollars, sterling and other assets as reserves is the consequence of the evolution of the international monetary system. At the end of 1968, the total reserves of all countries amounted to over $ 76 billion, with more than half in gold, about 40 per cent in foreign exchange, and the rest in the IMF gold tranche. The great objection to the old gold standard is that the amount available for monetary purposes fluctuates enormously. This can be seen once again in the experience of the postwar period. Output fell during the war and recovered very slowly. The growth of reserves was also held down by the large increase in private demand for industrial uses and traditional hoarding. In recent years, speculative purchases of gold increased so much that there was no rise in gold reserves from the end of 1964 to the third quarter of 1967 and a sharp fall in gold reserves in the last quarter of 1967 and the first quarter of 1968, the period of the gold crisis. The monetary gold stock may be regarded as virtually fixed at its present level of $ 41 billion.

The striking feature of the international monetary system is the dependence on dollars as a major reserve asset. Between 1950 and 1968, the increase in official holdings of dollars accounted for nearly one-half of the growth of total reserves. It is no longer possible to meet any significant part of the need for growth of reserves through deficits in the US balance of payments. At the same time, a large decline in official holdings of dollars would generate deflation in the world economy and undermine the international monetary system. The solution is to keep foreign exchange reserves at their present level by making them a fixed fiduciary reserve asset that cannot be increased or decreased.

Because there can no longer be a substantial increase in gold reserves and there should not be a substantial increase in foreign exchange reserves, the members of the IMF agreed to create a new reserve facility in the form of Special Drawing Rights. When the proposal is ratified and activated, all members of the IMF will be eligible for allocations of SDRs in proportion to their quotas. The amount of SDRs allocated should be conservative, say, at a rate of $ 2-2.5 billion in the initial five-year period. With the proper use of SDRs, the international monetary system would have a rational method of assuring an adequate growth of reserves to meet the trend needs of the world economy.

The great danger now is that the traditional preference for gold may induce countries to shift the composition of their reserves away from foreign exchange and SDRs to gold. The amendment on SDRs makes some provision for the proper use of all reserve assets. What is needed is a broader rule that would require countries to use their different reserve assets in the same ratios as they hold them. The simplest method of implementing such a rule would be to establish a Reserve Settlement Account in which participants would earmark their reserves and transfers or reserves would be made through debits and credits in a composite reserve unit (CRU). Title to the gold, foreign exchange and SDRs would remain with the countries earmarking the reserves. A Reserve Settlement Account would require no basic changes in the international monetary system. It would be a logical evolution of the gold standard.

Fixed parities and international reserves

In any international monetary system in which the values of national currencies are linked to each other through fixed parities, countries will hold reserves. Under the old gold standard that prevailed prior to World War I, the primary objective of economic policy was to maintain the gold value of the currency. The sole responsibility of governments in connection with exchange rates was the free coinage of gold (i.e., buying and selling gold for their currencies at a fixed price). Under the circumstances, gold was the only international reserve asset that the monetary authorities needed or held. The gold exchange standard came into wide use in the 1920's as a means of restoring exchange stability in countries that had abandoned the gold standard. At a time when there was widespread fear of a gold shortage, the gold exchange standard enabled countries to accumulate reserves while avoiding international competition for gold. The currencies held for this purpose were most conveniently dollars and sterling.

The present international monetary system is a form of the gold standard formalized in the statutes of the International Monetary Fund. While retaining the basic features of the gold standard, it permits countries greater flexibility in following domestic policies to achieve a high level of production and employment and sustained economic growth. Members of the IMF are required to define the parities of their currencies in terms of gold, or the dollar of the present gold content, and to maintain exchange rates for their currencies within 1 per cent of the agreed parity. However, a country can alter the parity of its currency after consultation and agreement with the IMF, if such a change is necessary to restore its balance of payments. Members are also required to establish convertibility of their currencies in accordance with the provisions of the statutes of the IMF.

To keep exchange rates within the prescribed range above and below parity, and to make their currencies convertible in fact, countries intervene in the exchange market, buying and selling their currencies for dollars when necessary.[1] For this purpose, all countries hold some reserves in dollars as minimum working balances and many countries hold the larger part of their reserves in this form. Sterling area countries hold most of their reserves in sterling, with the United Kingdom intervening

---

1. The United States is the only member of the IMF that has undertaken the obligation to maintain the exchange rates for its currency within the prescribed range by buying and selling gold to other monetary authorities for the settlement of international transactions. All other members have undertaken to maintain the dollar rates for their currencies in the exchange market, but not the obligation to do so by buying and selling gold.

to maintain the dollar-sterling exchange rate and indirectly the dollar rates of the currencies linked to sterling. The large trading countries of Europe, on the other hand, hold about twice as much of their reserves in gold as in foreign exchange. Changes in their gold reserves occur when they convert surplus dollars into gold or sell gold for dollars to restore their working balances, although they are affected by other transactions.[2]

Under the old gold standard, there was usually prompt adjustment of the balance of payments, mainly because the outflow and inflow of gold directly affected the money supply. Under the present system, countries are given more time to adjust their balance of payments in order to avoid harsh measures destructive of national or international prosperity. For this purpose, the IMF has large resources of gold and currencies (now about $ 21 billion) which are used to extend reserve credit to countries with payments deficits. As members have assured use of these resources up to the amount of their net creditor position in the IMF, such claims (the gold tranche) have many of the characteristics of reserves. Outside the IMF, large amounts of reserve credit are available through swap agreements and through *ad hoc* arrangements made by central banks in emergencies.

The holding of gold, dollars, sterling and other assets as reserves is the inevitable consequence of the evolution of the international monetary system. On the other hand, the amount of these assets held as reserves is partly the result of accidental forces that are not likely to recur. At the end of 1968, the total reserves of all countries outside the Communist group amounted to over $ 76 billion of which nearly $ 39 billion was in gold, just under $ 31 billion was in foreign exchange, and $ 6.5 billion was in net creditor claims on the IMF. Gold reserves increased sharply in the 1930's because of the devaluation of all currencies and the rise in the price of gold. Foreign exchange reserves increased considerably in the

---

2. The gold reserves of members of the IMF are reduced when they subscribe gold to the IMF, repurchase their currencies with gold, or pay charges in gold. Surplus countries whose currencies are needed by the IMF for extending reserve credit may acquire gold from the IMF through its purchases of their currencies.

1940's with the accumulation of sterling from the overseas military expenditures of the United Kingdom in World War II and even more in the 1950's and 1960's with the acquisition of dollars from the US balance of payments deficits. The gold tranche originated in the gold subscription to the IMF, which actually had no net effect on reserves, and increased considerably after 1964 because of large reserve credits extended by the IMF, particularly to the United Kingdom. The amount of reserves in the form of the gold tranche will fall as these reserve credits are repaid.

The strength and stability of the international monetary system require the solution of two reserve problems. The growth of aggregate reserve assets should be sufficient to provide countries with the means of financing deficits while they take corrective measures to restore their payments position without relying on deflation or trade and exchange restrictions. On the other hand, the growth of reserves should not be so plentiful, or in such a form, e.g., dollars, as to encourage countries to delay unduly the adjustment of their balance of payments. In effect, what is needed is an adequate but not excessive growth of reserve assets based on the trend needs of the world economy and completely separated from the behavior of the balance of payments of any country. The new reserve facility, Special Drawing Rights, is designed to meet this need.

Table VIII

INTERNATIONAL RESERVE ASSETS OF ALL COUNTRIES, 1968*
(Million dollars; end of year)

Gold in reserves of countries	38,925
(Gold held by international monetary institutions)	(1,969)
Foreign exchange reserves	30,865
(Dollars)	(17,470)
(Sterling)	(9,619)
(Other currencies)	(3,776)
Net creditor claims on the IMF (gold tranche)	6,488
Total, reserve assets of all countries	76,278

* Excludes the Communist countries; data are partly estimates.

There is a second reserve problem. In a world of multiple reserve assets—gold, dollars, other foreign exchange, and SDRs—it is essential to maintain their equivalence in international settlements. For traditional reasons, gold has always been the preferred reserve asset of the large trading countries. In recent years, gold has acquired a relative scarcity which has made it very difficult to maintain the equal attractiveness of gold and foreign exchange as reserve assets. The relative scarcity of gold will become even greater after the new reserve facility (SDRs) is activated. A method must be found for preventing the preference for gold from disrupting the orderly functioning of the international monetary system.

In considering the future role of the different reserve assets, it is necessary to make some assumptions regarding developments in the world economy. First, it is assumed that the great trading countries will succeed in restoring a well-balanced pattern of international payments. For the United States, this means a balanced position measured on an official reserve transactions basis. Second, it is assumed that this will be achieved within the framework of the Bretton Woods principles—that is, fixed parities which can be changed by agreement with the IMF. This would not preclude somewhat wider margins than 1 per cent above and below parity, but probably not more than 2 per cent. Finally, it is assumed that the international monetary system will remain essentially a gold standard system—that is, one in which currencies are defined in terms of gold at $ 35 an ounce, other reserve assets are linked in value to gold, and gold constitutes a major component of international reserves.

The future role of gold

The role of gold as a determinant of the behavior of the international monetary system will almost certainly continue to decline. Those who want a restoration of the old gold standard, with gold as the sole reserve asset, argue that this is the only way to maintain monetary discipline—that is, of avoiding inflation and securing prompt adjustment of the balance of payments. There is little doubt that in the hierarchy of economic objectives, monetary stability has been placed too low and that this has imparted an inflation bias to the world economy. The remedy for that is greater emphasis on monetary stability in policy making, not the return to an inflexible monetary system. The gold standard will not stop countries from following inflationary policies, if they are determined to do so, particularly if the inflation can be ratified by a subsequent rise in the monetary price of gold.

The old gold standard did not provide a monetary system free of inflation and deflation—no commodity money can do that. The great objection to the old gold standard, whether as the basis for a national monetary system or as the sole reserve asset in the international monetary system, is that the output of gold and the amount available for monetary purposes fluctuates enormously. This is evident in the data on gold production in the 75 years before World War I. To some extent countries could offset fluctuations in the output of gold through institutional changes that permitted a larger increase in the money supply than in gold reserves. Even so, they were confronted with prolonged periods of deflation and inflation arising from variations in gold production. Between 1896 and 1913, for example, the monetary gold stock of the United States increased from $ 527 million to $ 1,881 million and the index of

Table IX

PRODUCTION OF GOLD, QUINQUENNIEL PERIODS, 1841-1915

Period	Annual average output million dollars*	Period	Annual average output million dollars*	Period	Annual average output million dollars*
1841-1845	26.2	1866-1870	129.0	1891-1895	162.9
1846-1850	46.6	1871-1875	111.7	1896-1900	257.3
1851-1855	127.9	1876-1880	110.4	1901-1905	322.6
1856-1860	131.5	1881-1885	102.1	1906-1910	433.5
1861-1865	123.5	1886-1890	112.9	1911-1915	460.1

* At $ 20.67 a troy ounce.

wholesale prices rose by 50 per cent. In this period, during which the old gold standard acquired its greatest prestige, the inflation was twice as great as occurred in the United States between 1950 and 1968, despite the wars in Korea and Vietnam.

As shown by recent experience, gold is still a very unreliable means of securing a steady and adequate growth of international reserve assets. Gold production was stimulated in the 1930's by the Great Depression and the sharp rise in the price of gold. Output fell during the war and recovered very slowly after the war because of rising costs. Gold production outside the Communist countries did not reach the 1940 level ($ 1,264 million) again until 1962. Apart from South Africa, gold production in every producing country was less in 1968 than before the war. Total gold production has been on a plateau of just over $ 1.4 billion since 1965 and is as likely to fall as to rise. There is virtually no prospect that gold production will be sufficient, in view of private demand, to supply any significant addition to gold reserves in the future—not at $ 35 an ounce.

The growth of gold reserves has also been held down by the enormous increase in the private demand for gold for industrial uses and traditional hoarding, and more recently for speculation. From 1951 to 1955, private buyers absorbed about 50 per cent of gold production outside the Communist countries. From 1961 to 1964, private buyers absorbed close to 80 per cent of gold production. The consequence was that the increase in the stock of monetary gold between 1951 and 1964 varied from as little as $ 265 million in 1951 to as much as $ 820 million in 1963. The large year-to-year changes in the increase in the stock of monetary gold from 1951 to 1964 were due to a minor extent to the ebb and flow of speculation. The main reason for the irregular growth of gold reserves was the volatility of Soviet gold sales. In 1963 and 1964, for example, when the private absorption of gold was about $ 2.2 billion in the two years, the monetary gold stock nevertheless increased by $ 1,530 million because of Soviet gold sales of about $ 1 billion.

From the end of 1964 to the end of the third quarter of 1967, there was no increase whatever in the stock of monetary gold as all of the output plus the gold sales of the Soviet Union were absorbed by private buyers. This sudden increase in the private absorption of gold was due to speculative purchases averaging about $ 500 million a year. Following the devaluation of sterling in November 1967, gold speculation increased to such an extent as to precipitate a crisis. After having supplied nearly $ 3 billion of gold through the London market in the last quarter of 1967 and the first quarter of 1968, the central banks of the gold pool countries decided on March 17, 1968 to halt the sale of gold to private markets and to use gold only in transfers among the monetary authorities. Since then there has been a small increase in the stock of monetary gold.

The remarkable economic growth after World War II is due to many

Table X

GOLD PRODUCTION, SOVIET SALES, AND CHANGES IN MONETARY STOCK, 1951-68*
(Millions of dollars at $ 35 a fine troy ounce)

Year	Production	Soviet sales**	Change in monetary stock	Year	Production	Soviet sales**	Change in monetary stock
1951	827	...	265	1961	1,215	300	605
1952	852	...	230	1962	1,300	200	370
1953	849	75	455	1963	1,356	550	820
1954	897	75	670	1964	1,406	450	710
1955	944	75	665	1965	1,440	550	120
1956	979	150	485	1966	1,440	...	−45
1957	1,019	260	690	1967	1,410e	15	−1,580
1958	1,051	220	680	1968	1,450e	No estimate	−695
1959	1,127	300	755				
1960	1,178	200	295				

* All countries, except the Communist group, and international monetary institutions.
** Soviet gold sales are estimates.

factors. Nevertheless, it could not have occurred if the international monetary system had not provided a favorable environment for the tremendous expansion of international trade and investment. One aspect of this was the increase of reserves and their acquisition by the large trading countries of continental Europe. Gold, however, made very little contribution to the increase of reserves in this period. From the beginning of 1950 to the end of 1958, total international reserve assets increased from about $ 45.5 billion to about $ 76.3 billion—that is, at an average annual rate of 2.8 per cent. Of this increase only $ 5.5 billion was in gold. Including the gold holdings of international monetary institutions, the increase in the monetary gold stock was less than $ 6 billion—from $ 35 billion to about $ 40.9 billion. Under the circumstances, the international monetary system had to depend on other reserve assets, mainly dollars, to secure the necessary growth of international reserves.

The stock of monetary gold may be regarded as virtually fixed at its present level of just under $ 41 billion. The monetary authorities will not sell gold to the private market and the amount of newly-mined gold acquired by the monetary authorities will be very small. It is true that South Africa would like to sell some gold to the IMF at $ 35 an ounce; but the purpose undoubtedly is to establish the continued eligibility of newly-mined gold for incorporation in the monetary stock. With the price of gold in private markets at nearly $ 43 an ounce, it is unlikely that South Africa can derive a pecuniary advantage from selling gold to the monetary authorities in order to force up the price in private markets. It would be needlessly dogmatic for the IMF not to buy gold from South Africa under appropriate conditions. Such purchases would be little more than symbolic. They could make no significant contribution to the steady growth of reserves to meet the needs of the world economy.

The role of dollars and other foreign exchange

The striking feature of the evolution of the international monetary system in the last 18 years is the great dependence on the dollar as a major reserve asset. From the beginning of 1950 to the end of 1968, total foreign exchange reserves increased from about $ 10.4 billion to about $ 30.9 billion. As the holding of reserves in the form of sterling did not really increase in this period, apart from sterling acquired in swaps, by far the greater part of the addition to foreign exchange reserves was in dollars. From the beginning of 1950 to the end of 1968, the amount of dollars held as reserves by foreign monetary authorities increased by about $ 14.6 billion. The large increase in the holdings of other currencies as foreign exchange reserves was mainly in 1966, when sterling was weak, and again in 1968, during the European exchange crisis. The foreign exchange reserves in continental currencies are the result of swaps—that is, short-term reserve credit. The amount of reserves held in these currencies will decline sharply when the swaps are reversed.

The increase of reserves in the form of dollars was the result of the US balance of payments deficits and the willingness of countries to hold additional dollars rather than convert them into gold. Without the US deficits, the international monetary system would long ago have suffered from a serious shortage of reserves. In fact, some economists hold that the demand for reserves by other countries—gold, as well as dollars—helped to generate the US payments deficits, at least until 1965. In any case, it is no longer possible to continue to meet any significant part of the need for additional reserves through large and persistent deficits in the US balance of payments. At the same time, it would be dangerous to have a large decline in official holdings of dollars, for that would have serious consequences for the international monetary system and the world economy.

As this indicates, there is a practical limit to the amount of foreign exchange that can be held as international reserve assets and particularly to dependence on additions to foreign exchange as a means of meeting the need for the growth of reserves. That practical limit has been exceeded for sterling and it has about been reached for the dollar. One objection to further dependence on dollars for the growth of reserves is that the amount created is haphazard as it varies with the US balance of payments. Moreover, in a world with an inflation bias, it is illogical to offer any country, including the United States, the privilege of financing its deficits to an indefinite amount and for an indefinite time by incurring additional reserve liabilities. It is inconceivable that other large trading countries will continue to accumulate dollar reserves on a very large scale in exchange for their goods, services and capital assets.

There is an even more important objection to excessive dependence on foreign exchange as reserves. Foreign exchange is not a final reserve asset —that is to say, foreign exchange reserves are convertible into gold. This is not of consequence when the ratio of foreign exchange to gold is relatively small and confidence in the reserve currencies is very great. It can be of great consequence when foreign exchange reserves are about 40 per cent of total reserves, excluding claims on the IMF, confidence in currencies has been shaken by a series of crises, and the price of gold in private markets is at a high premium. The greatest threat to the international monetary system is the possibility of a flight by central banks from the dollar to gold. This would result in a sudden fall in aggregate reserves, possibly induce a deflation in the United States and the world

Table XI

OFFICIAL HOLDINGS OF FOREIGN EXCHANGE RESERVES, 1950-68
(Millions of dollars at parity rates)

	Total	Dollars	Sterling	Other currencies*
Jan. 1, 1950	10,390	2,910	7,480	
Dec. 31, 1958	16,950	9,648	6,698	604
Dec. 31, 1964	23,675	15,771	7,118	786
Dec. 31, 1965	23,195	15,849	7,112	234
Dec. 31, 1966	24,660	14,965	7,859	1,836
Dec. 31, 1967	28,255	18,303	8,256	1,696
Dec. 31, 1968	30,865e	17,470	9,619	3,776e

* Data on other currencies are derived as a residual.

economy, and probably undermine the existing structure of exchange rates which is based on the equivalence of the dollar and gold.

The common sense solution to this problem is to keep foreign exchange reserves at their present level by making them a fixed fiduciary reserve asset that cannot be increased or decreased. This would at the same time avert an unwanted continuation of US payments deficits merely to provide reserves, and the threat to international monetary stability from a large reduction in present holdings of dollars as reserves. A limitation on the further increase of foreign exchange reserves is the logical corollary of the creation of a new reserve facility to meet the trend need for additional reserves. The early activation of the Special Drawing Rights is necessary precisely because there can no longer be a substantial increase in gold reserves and there should no longer be a substantial increase in foreign exchange reserves.

An arrangement for making foreign exchange reserves a fixed fiduciary reserve asset would not involve a diminution of the role of the dollar in the actual operations of the international monetary system or the world economy. The monetary authorities would still hold dollars as working balances and they would use these dollars to intervene in the exchange market. Working balances would increase along with the growth of world trade. Of course, there would be no limitation on the holding and use of dollars to finance international trade and investment. In an expanding world economy, there will be a growing need for dollars to be held and used by banks and business firms throughout the world. The incomparably broad and liquid money and capital markets of the United States are of world-wide benefit. These markets must continue to perform their usual functions for the world economy. There is no reason why fixing the level of dollar reserves should diminish the growth of foreign private dollar holdings, either in the money markets of the United States or in the Eurodollar markets abroad.

Special Drawing Rights

The Group of Ten and the IMF gave long and careful consideration to alternative methods of supplementing gold and foreign exchange reserves. The proposal for Special Drawing Rights represents a consensus of different views on how a new reserve facility should be provided. At the meeting in Rio de Janeiro in September 1967, the Board of Governors of the IMF approved the submission of an amendment to the Articles of Agreement authorizing the creation and allocation of SDRs and making related changes in the present quota method of granting reserve credit. After the amendment is ratified, it will still be necessary to take a decision to activate the new reserve facility. This will be done on the recommendation of the Managing Director and with the approval of participants holding 85 per cent of the voting power. The same majority is required in deciding on the amount, the period, and the timing of allocations of SDRs.

All members of the IMF will be eligible to participate in the new reserve facility, and allocations of SDRs to each country will be proportionate to its IMF quota. Decisions to allocate SDRs will be made for basic periods of five years, although actual allocations within the agreed amount will be at shorter intervals perhaps quarterly. A country may opt not to participate in the allocations of any basic period. A participant will be entitled to use its SDRs to obtain an equivalent amount of a convertible currency from a country designated by the IMF. A participant must use its SDRs only to meet balance of payments needs or in the light of developments in its reserves, and not for the sole purpose of changing the composition of its reserves. By agreement, a country may also use SDRs to convert official balances of its currency held by another participant.

There are two quantitative limitations on the use of SDRs. A participating country that accepts SDRs is not required to hold them in excess of an amount equal to three times its cumulative allocations, although it may choose to do so. A participating country that uses SDRs must reconstitute its holdings so that five years after the first allocation, and quarterly thereafter, its holdings of SDRs in the five preceding years will average not less than 30 per cent of its cumulative allocations. Within these quantitative limitations, and despite their fiduciary character, the SDRs are final reserve assets in the sense that there is no obligation to convert them into gold. It might seem that the quantitative limitations on the use and holding of SDRs detract from their character as a reserve asset; but in fact they are best understood as a technique for requiring the use of other reserve assets as well as SDRs.

After the new reserve facility is activated the growth of reserve assets will be very largely in the form of SDRs. There will be no increase in gold reserves, except as South Africa decides to make token sales to the monetary authorities. Neither the United States nor other countries would want to see any substantial increase in dollar reserves once the new reserve facility is activated. Under the circumstances, primary reliance for the growth of reserve assets in the future will have to be placed on SDRs. Once it is clear that SDRs do function successfully as reserves, they may be expected to perform a gradually more important role in the international monetary system. To what extent and how soon SDRs will become a major reserve asset will depend on decisions still to be made on the activation and the rate of allocation of the new reserve facility.

On the whole, reasonable doubts regarding the amount of SDRs to be allocated should be resolved on the side of conservatism. Their status as a reserve asset, fully equivalent in acceptability to gold and dollars, can be established only by experience. Initially, while meeting the need for additional reserves, a conservative approach would assure a sufficient scarcity of SDRs so that they would be in fact a supplement to rather than a replacement of gold and dollars in international settlements. The present level of monetary reserves is probably not unduly large or small relative to the needs of the world economy; although with the serious deficiency of reserves in the United Kingdom and the less than adequate reserves in the United States and France, it is more likely that aggregate reserves are too little rather than too much. There is no need, however, for a massive initial infusion of SDRs as has been suggested.

On these considerations, the allocations of SDRs in the first basic period should be about $ 2 billion a year, although initial allocations of $ 2.5 billion a year would still be conservative. At this rate, annual allocations would be somewhat less than 3 per cent of total reserves at this time; and probably about 2.5 per cent of total reserves at the end of the first basic period. With allocations of $ 2 billion a year in the first basic period, the growth of aggregate reserves would be at about the same rate as from 1950 to 1968. This is certainly not too much, even for the first basic period, in view of the fact that the need for reserves between 1950 and 1968 was met by the redistribution of existing reserves as well as the growth of reserves. In subsequent periods, the amount of SDRs allocated could be substantially greater, provided the new reserve facility proves to be a constructive factor in balance of payments adjustments.

Even with a conservative rate of allocation, SDRs would soon be an important reserve asset. At $ 2 billion a year, the amount of SDRs outstanding after the first basic period of five years would be $ 10 billion. Assuming no increase in other reserve assets, SDRs would be about 12 per cent of aggregate reserves (including the present gold tranche)— that is, more than any other reserve asset except gold and dollars. After the second basic period, with allocations of $ 2.5 billion to $ 3 billion a year, the amount of SDRs outstanding would be close to 25 per cent of aggregate reserves—that is, not much less than the present amount of foreign exchange reserves although considerably less than reserves in the form of gold. As SDRs would provide nearly all of the increase in reserve assets in the future, they would be the principal determinant of the rate of growth of aggregate reserves. If SDRs are issued in proper amount, properly used, and properly integrated with other reserve assets, the international monetary system would for the first time have a rational method of assuring an adequate but not excessive growth of reserves to meet the trend needs of an expanding world economy.

Multiple reserve assets

The evolution of the international monetary system has resulted in a multiplicity of reserve assets. Excluding the gold tranche in the IMF, reserves wil be comprised of gold, dollars, other foreign exchange, and in the near future SDRs. In any system of multiple reserve assets, the orderly functioning of the system depends upon the use, without discrimination, of all forms of reserves in international settlements. The maintenance of the equivalence of all reserve assets is not a theoretical problem; it already exists. Many central banks have a traditional preference for gold, and this preference can no longer be satisfactorily overcome by the high interest rates paid on holdings of foreign exchange reserves. The premium on gold in private markets has added a new dimension to the preference for gold. The problem of maintaining the equivalence of all reserve assets could become even more acute after the activation of SDRs.

If the preference for gold as a reserve asset were to continue and intensify, it would prevent the orderly functioning of the international monetary system. At best, gold might come to be regarded as too valuable to be used in international settlements, so that in practice this part of the reserves would be immobilized—held as a traditional symbol rather than as useable reserves. At worst, central banks might systematically shift the composition of their reserve assets away from dollars, other foreign exchange, and SDRs to gold. In a world in which the stock of monetary gold is virtually frozen, this would lead to a competitive struggle in which some countries attempt to add to their gold reserves by cannibalizing the gold reserves of others. Such a disruptive preference for gold could in the end result in deflation or a breakdown in the Bretton Woods system of fixed parities. There is a real danger that the world economy might experience anew the exchange disorders of the 1930's which the IMF was designed to avoid.

The amendment on SDRs makes some provision for the proper use of all reserve assets. The basic principle, as noted, is that SDRs shall be used only to meet balance of payments needs and not for the sole purpose of changing the composition of a participant's reserve assets. The reconstitution provision (Schedule G) states that in the use of SDRs "participants shall also pay due regard to the desirability of pursuing over time a balanced relationship between their holdings of SDRs and their holdings of gold and foreign exchange and their reserve positions in the Fund." Schedule F states that in making transfers of SDRs for convertible currencies, the countries selected by the IMF "shall be designated for such amounts as will promote over time equality in the ratios of the participants' holdings of SDRs in excess of their net cumulative allocations to their official holdings of gold and foreign exchance." Clearly, the SDR amendment to the IMF statutes recognizes the importance of having countries use other reserve assets as well as SDRs in settlement of deficits and of having countries accept SDRs as well as other reserve assets in settlement of surpluses.

The problem of assuring the equivalence of all reserve assets in international settlements is actually much broader than the regulation of the use of SDRs. After all, foreign exchange reserves will continue to be much larger in amount than SDRs for more than a decade. The disruption that could occur in the international monetary system would be far greater if the preference for gold were to undermine the acceptability of foreign exchange reserves than if it simply involved discrimination in the use of SDRs. The various proposals that have been made for harmonization of the holding of reserve assets (notably that of Professor Posthuma) were a recognition of the danger arising from the growing preference for gold. The real problem, however, is not to achieve a harmonization in the holding of different reserve assets by the large trading countries, but to assure the balanced use of all reserve assets in international settlements.

There is no need, and it would be impossible in practice, to reverse the historical forces that have resulted in the creation of different reserve assets and their distribution according to the traditions and preferences of the monetary authorities of various countries. What is needed now is a rule that would require the use of all reserve assets—in whatever form they are held—in a non-discriminatory manner in all international

settlements. An equitable rule would have to embody two principles:
1. Each deficit country should use its different reserve assets in settlement of its deficit in precisely the same ratios as it holds these reserves—gold, foreign exchange, and SDRs.
2. Each surplus country should acquire the different reserve assets in settlement of its surplus in the average ratios of gold, foreign exchange, and SDRs used by the deficit countries, so that all surplus countries would acquire the different reserve assets in precisely the same ratios.

It should be emphasized again that such a rule would not harmonize the present composition of reserves—it is specifically designed not to do so. It would, however, harmonize the composition of the increment of reserves that surplus countries acquire. In order to avoid changing the existing composition of reserves through the accidental timing of surpluses and deficits, settlement in the different reserve assets would have to be on a cumulative basis. Thus, a country that has a deficit in one year and an equal surplus in a subsequent year would have the same composition of reserves as if it had maintained a balanced payments position throughout the period. As it would not be practical to require countries to transfer a mixed bag of gold, dollars, other foreign exchange, and SDRs every time they find it necessary to use reserves, provision would have to be made for a single transfer of a reserve claim that would automatically have the effect of making settlement in the different reserve assets in the appropriate ratios.

Reserve Settlement Account

The simplest method of implementing the rule on the equitable use of all reserve assets would be for the members of the IMF to establish a Reserve Settlement Account through which transfers of reserves would be made. Each participating member would put its different reserve assets on earmark with the Reserve Settlement Account and would be credited on its books with the total of its earmarked reserves denominated in a composite reserve unit (CRU). The composition of the CRU would be different for each country, depending on the precise reserve assets it placed on earmark. The value of the CRU would be the same for all countries, regardless of the precise reserves they earmarked with the Reserve Settlement Account; and it would be defined as $\frac{1}{35}$ of an ounce of gold—the present gold value of the dollar and the unit of value for the SDRs. As the reserves would be earmarked rather than deposited, title to the reserve assets would remain with the country, the Reserve Settlement Account acting merely as an administrator for recording the transfer of reserves.

Transfers of reserves between countries, say, to acquire dollars or other convertible currencies to be used in the exchange market, would be made by debiting the earmarked account of one country and crediting the earmarked account of another country for the amount of CRUs involved in the reserve transactions. No actual transfer of the different reserve assets would be made from one earmarked account to another, although the implicit transfers would be shown by the increase or decrease of a country's balance in the Reserve Settlement Account compared with the total amount of reserves it placed on earmark.

If desired, the Reserve Settlement Account could be established by having countries earmark a minimum proportion of their reserves in precisely the same ratio as their holdings of different reserve assets. Furthermore, if desired, cumulative surplus countries could have returned to them a part of the reserves they earmarked with the Reserve Settlement Account after their net position in CRUs is sufficiently large. The return of reserves to surplus countries would be in the same ratios as they placed on earmark. Similarly deficit countries would have to replenish their position in CRUs after their balances become depleted; but the additional reserves they earmark would have to be in the same ratios as their holdings of different reserve assets. A final settlement on the basis of the cumulative surplus or deficit of a country would be made whenever it withdraws from the Reserve Settlement Account.

Countries that earmark gold in the Reserve Settlement Account could retain physical possession of the gold at their own central bank or at any depository of the IMF. The gold would remain the specific asset of that country and it could be shown in the accounts of the central bank. The only change that would occur in its gold reserves would be that arising from the obligation to make settlement *pro rata* in gold and other reserve assets if it is a cumulative deficit country or to receive gold *pro rata* with other reserve assets if it is a cumulative surplus country. Participants in the Reserve Settlement Account would not buy or sell gold as such. The Reserve Settlement Account would, however, be permitted to buy newlymined gold from participating countries at $ 35 an ounce, paying for it with CRUs. The General Account of the IMF would also earmark the gold it holds, receiving an equivalent amount of CRUs which it could use in its reserve credit operations in the same way as it now uses gold.

Countries would also earmark their dollars, sterling, and other foreign exchange with the Reserve Settlement Account. These foreign exchange assets would be transferred by the Reserve Settlement Account to the reserve centers in return for non-negotiable demand notes whose value would be guaranteed in terms of the CRU and which would bear an agreed rate of interest. Countries would retain working balances in foreign exchange, but would not acquire any additional reserves in this form. Thus, the present amount of foreign exchange would become a fixed fiduciary reserve asset held on earmark with the Reserve Settlement Account, but could not be increased or decreased. Central banks would be permitted to engage in swaps, as such operations are a form of reserve credit and do not really involve the creation of reserves. There would be no limitation, of course, on the growth of private holdings of dollars, including those of private banks.

Holdings of SDRs would also be earmarked with the Reserve Settlement Account. This would involve no change in the contemplated practice, as such reserve assets will in any case be held in the Special Account of the IMF with transfers recorded on its books. In fact, the Reserve Settlement Account may be thought of as extending to the holding and use of other reserve assets the same techniques established in the Amendment of the IMF statutes for the holding and use of SDRs. There is one difference, however, between SDRs and other reserve assets—the amount earmarked with the Reserve Settlement Account would increase whenever a participant receives a new allocation. The paying and receiving of interest on SDRs would be as provided in the Amendment; and the same principle could be applied to paying and receiving interest on the foreign exchange earmarked with the Reserve Settlement Account.

A Reserve Settlement Account would require no basic changes in the international monetary system which would remain a form of the gold standard. The parities of currencies would be denominated in gold, and exchange rates would fluctuate within a limited range above and below parity. Reserve assets would consist of gold, dollars, other foreign exchange, and later SDRs. Balance of payments settlements would be made in reserves, with deficit countries using their different reserve assets *pro rata*, and surplus countries acquiring the different reserve assets in the average ratios in which they are used by deficit countries. The only new feature would be the earmarking of reserve assets with the Reserve Settlement Account and the transfer of reserves through debits and credits denominated in a composite reserve unit (CRU) with a fixed value of $ 1 in gold.

This is a natural evolution of the gold standard. Once the SDRs are activated, it will be possible to have an orderly growth of monetary reserves based on the trend needs of the world economy, rather than remain dependent for reserves on the uncertainties of gold production and gold speculation or continuing deficits in the balance of payments of the reserve centers. The Reserve Settlement Account would be the simplest way of assuring the balanced use of all reserve assets in international settlements. It is probably not too much to say that the only way the gold standard can survive is by adapting it to the needs of the world economy —through activation of the SDRs and the establishment of a Reserve Settlement Account.

Chapter V

DEVELOPING COUNTRIES AND THE INTERNATIONAL MONETARY SYSTEM

SELECTED ISSUES

by *Javier Márquez*

Introduction

There is no such thing as a less-developed country (LDC) position regarding the world monetary system and its working. On some of the basic issues there is no more unanimity among the less-developed countries than there is among the industrialized ones. Not only this, but—in contrast to the situation in the latter—there is a frequent lack of consistency in the positions adopted by individual LDCs in different forums, a contrast which is particularly apparent when comparing the stands taken at UNCTAD with those taken at the Annual Meetings of the IMF, where they may even not adopt any position at all. This could probably be explained by a combination of less internal coordination in the LDCs, that is, the absence of *a* national policy, the fact that in the IMF there is no caucus of the developing countries, the different personalities involved, their relative inhibitions and interests, etc.

In this chapter I have tried, in specific cases, to interpret the LDCs' attitudes. No judgment is passed on the importance for them of the international monetary system relative to other international economic issues.

Furthermore, I assume that the development of developing countries is a problem of paramount importance for the industrialized ones, a reality which cannot be simply wished away. Such a development is in the short and long run (in the self-interest) of the industrial countries and they should act accordingly. I also take the position that the international monetary game should not be an even one, that the industrial heavyweights should, by common agreement, give a handicap to the developing featherweights. The international monetary game concerns everybody, but the players are not of equal size. Moreover, the international monetary game is a part of *one* big international economic game which cannot, or should not, be divided into several unconnected parts, each one with its own rules. There cannot, or should not, be one policy of the industrial countries towards the developing ones in the field of trade, another and a different one in the field of capital movements, still another in the field of liquidity, etc.

The world monetary system and its management

That the present international monetary system is not accepted as the final goal by either the industrial or the LDC countries is proved by the insistent complaints and plans for further change which are mushrooming as a result of all the gaps left in the recent, and still unimplemented reform, as well as because of its insufficient international social orientation.[1] In fact, our present system can claim in its favour mainly the respectability of tradition, of old things. The situation will not change sufficiently, as to its basic philosophy, with the reform. The ideal system would be a wisely managed technically and socially oriented one, a system that would punish the sinful inflationists—or inflations of sinful origin—help to restore equilibrium, promote growth throughout the world and favour a better income distribution between countries.

The difficulty in reaching such a desideratum derives not so much, I believe, from deficiencies in economic thinking or lack of technical competence as from the current unacceptability of a man-managed system. This is the result of a dogged insistence on national financial sovereignty and of mutual distrust. In the absence of an acceptable man-managed

---

1. Antisocially and socially oriented are meant throughout this paper in the same sense that an income tax proportional to income is antisocial and a progressive income tax is socially oriented.

system, one will have to cope for a long time with commonly agreed automatic, or semi-automatic rules on some of the essential points, try to orient them socially, and strive to get closer and closer to a wise management in those aspects which lend themselves less to automaticity.

There is probably no difference in this respect between industrial and developing countries. The former will not accept a man-managed system because they do not trust other industrial countries, either economically or politically, while the developing countries would not accept it because they distrust not only some other developing countries but all, most, or some of the industrialized ones as well. They also know that a man-managed international monetary system would most probably mean one fully managed by the larger industrial countries. On this point the industrial countries have left nothing to the imagination.

The evolution should, then, be—this is my preference—in the sense of an increase of the social orientation of automaticity of the agreed rigid rules or formulae whenever automaticity is viable, and of a decreasing automaticity provided there are sufficient guarantees that the developing countries will be given a substantial handicap when it comes to policy decisions.

One of the points on which the developing countries have had contrasting opinions concerns the role of the IMF as the institutional center of the world monetary system, as well as the breadth of its activities. It is my impression that the last five or six years have seen a great change in this respect. There was a time when a number of developing countries probably shared the opinions of the UNCTAD group of experts on international liquidity, in the sense that the issue and the management of a new reserve asset should not be entrusted to the IMF, which is to say that such countries would have preferred to reduce the Fund's role in the world monetary system. What turned the tide was probably the haughty attitude of the Group of Ten at the time when some of its members would openly say that liquidity was their exclusive field, followed by the reaction of the Management of the Fund itself asserting that liquidity was the concern of every country (and the business of the Fund), that developing countries needed liquidity as much as the industrialized ones. No doubt, the increasingly liberal Fund policies, as well as its proof of concern for the LDCs—e.g. with the establishment of the compensatory financing scheme—also helped. The developing countries saw in the IMF a friendly agency, at least a much friendlier one than the Ten, taken as a group. So, instead of a new machinery over which the developed countries would have had a still larger control, the developing countries stood by the Fund as the agency empowered to create SDRs.

All this being said, I think there is a feeling that the IMF cannot be considered the ideal setting for a wisely man-management, socially oriented, international monetary system under its present structure. Improvements are needed and should be viable.

Against the present background, the voting privileges of industrial countries stand out, that is to say their individual voting power and the majority requirements, both of which have frequently been of concern to the LDCs. Although some industrial countries still consider that their strength in the IMF is insufficient relative to other developed ones, which may be true (and I have nothing against the improvement of individual countries' positions in the IMF as their relative fortunes evolve), I also think that the objective criteria for the establishment of the voting power of Fund members—even as amended by the additional votes given to countries as such—do not take sufficiently into account the special privileges that the developing countries should receive in the international monetary game. True, many developing countries realize that their situation in this respect is just another example of the facts of power, which they should try to erode—that is, they should try to give to this sort of automaticity a better social orientation—but with which they will have to live as long as, and to the extent that they continue to exist.

It has been suggested in a Latin American country that the IMF could be regionalized, in the sense of having in the Fund representatives of countries from specific developing regions (Latin America, Africa, the Middle East, etc.). These national representatives would meet with their Executive Directors and discuss the problems of special interest to them, prior to Executive Board Meetings, and would also review the Board's decisions from a regional point of view. The purpose of this proposal is to increase the developing countries' moral influence in the Fund to facilitate the acceptance of Fund decisions in the individual countries, and to appraise better, from their point of view the policies of other regions or countries, thus helping to improve world-wide policy coordination. Whatever the merits of this plan may be, it shows the concern of some developing countries over their influence in the IMF, and a genuine desire to have a widely accepted decision-making center in world monetary affairs.

I am also impressed by the implicit or explicit insistence of developing countries that the IMF is not close enough to the agencies that specialize in favouring their interests, whether these be world-wide and regional development financing agencies or world-wide and regional research and policy ones. It seems to me, on the basis of the available evidence, that developing countries would feel better protected against the dominant influence of the industrial ones in the world monetary system if they had more assurance that the Fund was more strongly influenced by such agencies, and that they would prefer an IMF capable of using its available resources (not necessarily from quotas and net income only) in conjunction with other agencies to the best interests of the world economy, and not constrained in its field of operations by obsolete ideas regarding its "proper field".[2]

It is easier said than done. Institutional relations have never been easy, and the developing countries have had sad experiences with their own agencies. It is also necessary to break the obstinate resistance of some countries to bringing together things they consider should be kept separate. I confess I do not at this moment have a plan with any sex appeal, or one that would be negotiable, but it should not be beyond human ingenuity to devise one if there were a real desire to have it.

---

2. During the last, 1968, IMF Annual Meeting, there were several criticisms of the IMF report on the stabilization of commodity prices, because it seemed to be oriented excessively towards what the Fund itself could do. The Latin American countries have also expressed the hope that the IMF might have direct financial dealings with regional agencies as such.

The problem seems to me of the utmost importance, for it is quite possible that the LDCs would be more likely to accept a decision-making center in the world monetary system if they were sufficiently confident that their interests in it were protected through the influence of known friendly agencies of high standing, in addition to their own representatives and that the center of the system was empowered to expand its activities directly or jointly with other agencies.

The adjustment process

The need for an accepted authority is especially acute in the field of the adjustment process. This is one side of the international monetary system in which the developing countries feel less protected at the present time. They rightly fear the policy decisions which may be taken unilaterally by the industrial countries, and still more those which may be commonly agreed by them. These policies may have far-reaching consequences for the LDCs, who as things are do not really have an opportunity to plead their case effectively at the right time.

The Annual Reports of the IMF and the opening addresses of its Managing Director are frequently very explicit as regards the consequences of the policies of industrial countries for its less-developed members. Moreover, on the occasion of such meetings the latter have packed their speeches with complaints about terms of trade, prices of primary goods, restrictive trade policies, the results of the Kennedy Round, too much use of monetary and not enough of fiscal policies—that is, high interest rates in industrial countries—difficult access to money and capital markets, tied loans, discrimination against certain countries or regions, inadequate aid, instability of reserve currencies, lack of parallelism in the adjustment process of surplus and deficit countries, and so on and so forth. These are complaints which the industrial countries obviously knew would be made when they adopted the policies that led to them.

The IMF has very little statutory authority in the adjustment process.

The only pertinent provision in its Articles of Agreement, the scarce currency clauses, will no doubt continue to be a mere remainder of the existence of the problem. Furthermore, the founding fathers established the performance criteria of the Fund members on the basis of current account transactions without going into the problem of capital movements, which is of vital importance for developing countries. Even in regional bodies, such as the OECD, this side of the issue still remains unfinished business, "longed bogged down in legalistic disputations over the preliminary terms of a tentative 'code of good behaviour', and now languishing in 'Working Party 3', although the OECD staff has done the best research and analytical work that is available on many of the ingredients of the problem."[3]

International financial discipline of one sort or another—depending on the situation of individual countries—designed to bring the balance of payments into equilibrium in the shortest tolerable time and without harm to third—mainly developing—countries is an integral part of a good international monetary system. Yet it has not been tackled properly, if at all, at the world level. The opportunity was missed—deliberately, I believe—on the occasion of the reform of the Charter of the IMF, and this in spite of the fact that the reform was stimulated largely by the alleged deficiencies in the adjustment process, and that the implementation of the SDRs was considered to be dependent upon the elimination of the US balance of payments deficit.

Let me hasten to add that, in this field, the developing countries would, or should, have accepted practically any method under which the IMF, whatever the relative influence of the industrial countries, would have had a say, for they could not possibly be worse off than at present. Today they are the mercy of the unilateral or commonly agreed goodwill of the industrial nations who, no doubt with the usual exceptions, have not shown much of it, or have not shown it in a non-discriminatory way.

---

3. Robert V. Roosa, "The world capital shortage—as seen from the United States", statement in the *Sesquincentennial Symposium of Brown Brothers, Harriman and Co.*, in Sun Valley, Idaho, September 18, 1968.

Besides, paternalism or political favours can hardly be considered the right solution.

The problem of financial coordination remains unsolved at all levels, as proven by the frequent complaints of the industrial nations as regards important policy measures taken without prior consultation. But they have the machinery, however imperfect, for such consultation, and it seems to have worked sometimes. There is ample evidence, however, that they prefer to deal with the LDCs bilaterally, a task in which they may at times be aided by some of those countries who consider themselves in a better bargaining position individually than collectively.

The extension of the network of bilateral or multilateral arrangements between industrialized countries to help each other out of more or less transitory balance of payments difficulties is another reason for uneasiness. The more such arrangements proliferate, the smaller will be the chances of the LDCs being taken into account, or of being heard, on the adjustment process of the industrial nations. The suspicion may be there, justified or not, that the lending, standbying, or swaping countries may agree among themselves not to hurt each other with their adjustment policies whatever the consequences for the rest of the world may be.[4]

I can readily understand the reluctance of *any* country to have its

---

4. This consideration has led, in Latin America, to the suggestion that the industrial countries should be pressed to increase their quotas in the IMF. It has been said that, in addition to improving the Fund's liquidity, this would induce those countries to seek their liquidity from the IMF, and this, in turn, would give the developing countries a chance of being heard on the adjustment policies of the industrial nations. While I am very much in favour of increasing the industrial countries' quotas in the IMF (except for its possible consequences for the issue of SDRs), I do not think that such a device could, *per se*, improve the chances of developing countries of influencing the policies of the industrial ones, for it would not compel them to take money from the Fund in the credit tranches instead of negotiating among themselves. Unless countries are brought into the Fund—in the way in which a commercial bank is brought into the central bank by forcing it to rediscount—the Fund has little authority over them. This is probably one of the reasons why, even at times when the Fund's supply of convertible currencies has been

prospective policies discussed in a large forum, however closed the doors are. The time is not ripe for it. But, to the extent that they are discussed at all by the industrial countries, some way should be found to introduce into the discussion the developing countries' side of the story. Since it cannot be done directly by the LDCs, as this would mean a crowded audience, the only alternative is to appraise it through a commonly agreed intermediary, preferably an IMF in which the LDCs had more statutory influence of one sort or another, although it could be also UNCTAD.

No doubt it would also be very desirable to start a process of gradual increase of the IMF authority on specific financial policy issues, that is, to start experimenting with a man-managed international monetary (financial) system.

The need for reserves

One of the most nonsensical things said about developing countries in relation to the problem of international liquidity is that higher reserves are a luxury that developing countries cannot afford, and that they do not need a high level of reserves, but instead need development financing. I believe that their need for reserves, relative to their trade or international payments, is higher than that of industrialized countries. It is my impression that this fact, together with the difficulties foced by the LDCs in building up their reserves, has been in some sense recognized by the creation of such a mechanism as the IMF plan for compensatory financing and by the IBRD proposal for supplementary financing. No doubt the LDCs also need development financing also, but it is not a question of reserves versus development financing, but of both of them, and it would be very unfair to argue that they have to choose between one or the other.

---

sufficient, several industrial countries have preferred to keep out of the credit tranches and have, instead, concluded *ad hoc* arrangements among themselves.

It must be admitted that some developing countries have at times expressed preference for development financing over reserves and even accepted that liquidity is mainly the concern of and of interest to industrial countries. This is absurd. Some of the reasons why the LDCs need a high level of reserves are not dissimilar from those that justify a high level of reserves for industrialized countries and some are more peculiar to the developing ones. Let me list some of them.

1. There is a whole body of arguments which relate to the structure of the LDCs' exports, imports and foreign debt: (*a*) As is well known, primary goods are subject to large and sharp price and demand fluctuations and they constitute an overwhelming part of developing countries' exports. Consequently, the frequently-voiced point that the larger foreign trade is, the greater the possibility of fluctuations in exchange receipts, which applies to all countries, applies still more to the developing ones. Whatever the marginal increase of reserves desirable for industrialized countries relative to an increase in their foreign trade might be, such an increase would be larger in the case of developing ones. (*b*) As shown by the composition of their imports, it is more difficult for the LDCs than for the industrialized countries to compress theirs without depressing their standard of living and impairing the process of development; in the case of several of the more developed of the LDCs which have gone through the preliminary stages of industrialization, a shortage of foreign exchange may also mean unemployment in those industries which use sizable amounts of imported raw materials and intermediate goods. (*c*) The servicing of the foreign debt, both private and public, is also an extremely rigid, and sometimes large, component of developing countries' foreign payments, and large reserves are needed to meet such a service when exports or capital receipts contract.

We have, thus, on top of the general need for reserve increases as the economies and trade grow, the additional need due to the sharper fluctuations in exchange receipts together with a greater rigidity of exchange payments. The ratio of reserves to foreign payments should thus be larger in developing than in industrialized countries.

2. Another series of arguments concerns confidence in the currency and access to development financing: (*a*) A high reserve breeds confidence in the currency, both in industrialized and in developing countries. I know of no developing country, or perhaps I should say Latin American country, where the authorities have not brought to the public eye a comfortable level of reserves, or where they have not felt extremely uneasy at the public's reaction to an uncomfortably low one. A low level of reserves stimulates speculative assaults on the currency, either for precautionary or profit motives. In this respect one can argue that the LDCs are not very different from the industrialized countries, but (*b*) lack of confidence in the currency resulting from a low level of international reserves, or from other causes, has for the developing countries a direct impact upon their level of investments. While domestic investable capital which would be available for investments under normal conditions leaves the country, it is more difficult to obtain foreign capital resources in the market (that is, without strings attached). I am convinced that, in developing countries, the investment foregone because of the accumulation of reserves is smaller, much smaller, than the investments that are not made when the reserves are considered too low.

3. A third group of arguments has to do with development policies and the flexibility of policy. (*a*) While I am a firm believer in financial stability as one of the requisites for development, I also believe that there is no such thing as a conservative development policy. Developing countries following an active development policy should have as expansionary financial policies as is compatible with economic stability, but no amount of economic know-how, programming, and so forth, will guarantee a country pursuing an active and, let us hope, bold development policy that its well-considered ambitions do not exceed its capacity. Accordingly, countries aiming at a high rate of growth have to follow a trial-and-error method in order to find out the extent of their capacity for development. If they err they should err rather on the ambitious side. Whether a development policy is excessively or insufficiently ambitious will be reflected in the reserve position. Clearly, a country with low reserves cannot afford

errors on the expansion side. (*b*) It has been argued, for example at UNCTAD, that low reserves mean that countries have to go continuously to foreign lenders for resources, and this deprives their economic policies of the necessary or advisable flexibility, for it places economic policy, so to speak, in foreign hands.

4. The LDCs' greater need for liquidity, their own reserves, also derives from their smaller access to borrowed reserves in world markets or to *ad hoc* arrangements. Developing countries have not benefited from such devices as swap arrangements, the issue of special bonds, massive collective central banks standby arrangements, etc., which have been so much heralded as a proof that we have entered a new era of international financial collaboration. They have relied more on their own reserves (and, no doubt, on access to international agencies, which are also open to the industrial countries).[5]

No doubt the above arguments in favour of a high level of reserves for developing countries do not apply equally to all of them, but I believe it would be difficult to find any developing country in which one or more would not be valid.

My position, accordingly, is that, unless some more fundamental changes occur in the world financial system, the LDCs should try to build up their reserves. Many of the arguments advanced to that effect also underline the difficulties which they encounter today, and will continue to face in the future, in the road to such a goal.

---

5. In the case of Latin America, it has also been said that it is the only large group of developing countries that does not reserve preferential financial treatment in the money and capital markets of one or other of the industrialized nations. This is not to say they should seek privileges, for they may be too expensive.

The distribution of new reserve assets

Since the beginning of international discussions on the creation of a new reserve asset, there has seemed to be agreement, at the official level, that the desirable increase of liquidity should be in accordance with "world needs", that is, independent of the needs of individual countries, whether developing or industrialized. Now, I have never been able to reach a level of abstraction which allows me to differentiate between the world's and individual countries' need for liquidity. The world needs more liquidity because all or some countries have insufficient reserves—or, we could say today, liquid reserves. In fact, to differentiate between world and countries' needs seems to me to be a *contradictio in terminis*, for, at least in this particular case, the problems of the whole must reflect the problem of its parts.

An economist from a developing country is apt to think that the Group of Ten countries would not have taken as much trouble as they did to devise a new reserve asset if they had not feared that *they* could run short of liquidity in the near future, and/or if some of them had not considered that they were already short of it, with little prospect of "earning" additional reserves. There is, I believe, ample evidence that the increase of *world* liquidity would not satisfy the industrial deficit-countries if it should happen through an increase of the reserves of the LDCs. As early as 1962 Per Jacobsson said, at that year's Annual Fund Meeting, that although many of the developing countries "would be wise to pay some attention to building up their reserves to a safer level, whatever efforts may be made by them to do so will presumably not cause any appreciable difficulties *from a general liquidity point of view*."[9] The liquidity of the LDCs was not considered a part of general liquidity! Other, perhaps less direct, examples of the same "theory" are not lacking.

The obvious difficulty lies in how to provide liquidity continuously in the amounts needed by countries which are deficient in reserves and are consequently following contractionist policies harmful to themselves and

---

6. IMF, *Summary Proceedings*, Annual Meeting, 1962, p. 26. My emphasis.

to others, while avoiding the possible, and much feared, inflationary consequences of an excessive provision—that is, in excess of world needs. Moreover, the shortage of reserves of individual countries is not always independent of policies, whether they are wise or foolish, and if the "illegitimate" liquidity needs are satisfied they are likely to persist, and new illegitimate needs may arise, all of which would lead to an inflationary spiral throughout the world. This is well-explored ground and leads to the rejection of any automatic mechanism for the creation of liquidity according to the "needs" of individual countries. I do not think that anybody has ever proposed the creation of such a monster, although some of Prof.Triffin's ideas have been misinterpreted in that sense.

The fact remains that, for the provision of new liquidity to serve its purpose, or to serve it better, it should be injected into the system at the points at which it is most needed, where it would, consequently, add more (directly or indirectly) to healthy world-wide expansion and growth, which to me includes a faster and healthier growth of the developing countries. If these were to receive the additional liquidity to that extent—not in excess of world needs—one could hardly speak of an inflationary excess of liquidity.

But somebody would have to judge which are the needy and deserving countries, the extent of their individual needs, and the policies which would allow a country to qualify as a deserving one. Apparently, nobody wants such a system at this moment, and there is little difference between developing and industrial countries in this respect. So one is left with the necessity for an arbitrary, automatic, way of injecting new liquidity into the system.

These lengthy considerations are meant to point out: (*a*) that developing countries should, for the time being, accept as a fact of life the system of prior decision on the total amount of liquidity to be created periodically, regardless of whether individual needs are legitimate or not; (*b*) that the amount of new liquidity to be created should be judged by the needs of individual countries, for there is no such a thing as an abstract "world need", although the world may be harmed by an excessive provision of liquidity to individual countries; and (*c*) that although the system of distribution of SDRs had to be arbitrary, since a logical one proved to be unacceptable, the one actually decided on can claim very little in its favour. If it had to be a mechanical, automatic system of distribution, it need not have been internationally antisocial.

Like the industrial countries, many LDCs have advocated for years a distribution of new liquidity on the basis of "objective criteria", and expressed preference for the quotas in the IMF as the fairest way of allocation. This position was adopted by the well-known report of the UNCTAD experts, very forcefully supported in this respect (among others) by the governments of the developing countries. The same position was adopted by the CIAP group of experts, in which I participated, and subsequently I held the same opinion on other occasions. Although several voices were heard in favour of a better solution, one finds numerous statements of developing countries to the same effect at the annual meetings of the IMF.

It is difficult to complain after having been given satisfaction on this very important matter. My interpretation today is that many of us were guilty of having been too eager to get into the liquidity receiving game, and afraid of being left entirely out of it. This was probably due to the cavalier way in which the outsiders were treated until 1966 by the exclusive Group of Ten. The rationale, or the economics, of the problem gave way to negotiability; what seemed possible, or attainable, was built up into a reasonable solution. There is one instance in the 1967 IMF Meeting in which a developing country openly expressed the gratitude due to the Group of Ten for the solution to which it consented.

So, we are in the game. But now the irrationality of the decision which was taken has become clearer, for the mechanical distribution of liquidity could have been made to conform more closely to "the liquidity needs of the world" by making it more favourable to the developing countries.

It is difficult now to see what is the rationale of giving more liquidity to the richer countries whether they are in deficit or not, and whatever the level of their reserves. Moreover, many doubts have been cast on whether, because of the quotas of SDRs which will eventually be allocated to them, industrial countries will follow more liberal trade, monetary and aid policies than they would otherwise have followed. If history is any guide to the future, we have the fact that the annual increase of reserves of all countries other than the United States between 1950 and 1968 was of the order of 5.6 per cent, and that of the other industrial countries much larger. This did not stimulate much liberality towards LDCs, which cannot really expect much from the indirect effects of the new liquidity assigned to the industrial nations, and these indirect effects were the main benefits which the latter assumed that the LDCs would derive from the reform.

Would it not have been more logical to assign all or most of the new liquidity to developing countries, perhaps—in the absence of a more acceptable criterion—according to their quotas in the IMF? *World* liquidity would certainly increase by the same amount whatever the distribution of a fixed quantity of SDRs, and the larger the proportion going to the LDCs the better the social orientation of the distribution.

Of course, one aspect of the international controversy prior to the decision to create SDRs, and of the clash between industrial and developing countries, was the rejection by most of the members of the first group of any system under which the new liquidity to be created could give rise to transfers of real resources, especially long-term transfers.

The point that such transfers had been the only way to acquire liquidity in the past and that, accordingly, there was no reason to reject them in the future, had little or no impact on the industrial countries. The increasingly accepted practice of national financial institutions receiving short-term funds and lending them at long-term, as well as the historical experience of the UK investing long-term all over the world the short-term foreign funds received in London, was not accepted as respectable arguments prior to the Rio de Janeiro IMF Meeting.

It is probably because of the passion with which many of the negotiators of the Group of Ten rejected the idea of *directly* linking the creation of liquidity with the financing of economic development and the long-run transfer of real resources that the developing countries, even in UNCTAD, generally speaking took refuge in a non-functional indirect link. Some of them argued, at IMF meetings, that the link was desirable *in spite of the fact* that development financing and liquidity were two different things; others, which had in UNCTAD supported the UNCTAD proposals, preferred to keep their mouths shut at the IMF, perhaps in order to improve the chances of the issue of new liquidity.

Acceptance of the long-term transfer of real resources as the right method of increasing liquidity, and of the conceptual and historical link between reserve creation and development financing, would certainly have led to a far more logical mechanical system of distribution of SDRs, in which the injection of new liquidity would have been *less* arbitrary, and which would have promoted the purposes for which SDRs are designed far better than the system already decided on.

France has for many years been in favour of a link between liquidity creation and development, although perhaps a very special one. At the last IMF Annual Meeting, Italy said the link had always existed. The UK has said, at a recent ECOSOC meeting, that the idea of a link has merits. These are probably not the only industrial countries holding the same opinion. Why, then, during the negotiating process, did the idea not gather sufficient "big countries" support to influence the decision?

The system *has* been decided, however, and there is no chance of changing it for several years to come. Yet some ideas expressed after the Rio Meeting both by less-developed and by industrialized countries prove that there are, within the established system, ways of achieving *some* of the same purposes for which developing countries were pressing before it. The main proposal, sponsored by UNCTAD at its last conference, consists of an agreement among and/or a pledge by industrial countries to make available for development financing, out of their reserves and through international agencies, mainly IDA, the equivalent of a certain proportion of the SDRs which they may receive.

That such a proposal has the support of some surplus industrialized countries is a healthy development. It is my hope that something of that sort will be done, although it can hardly be considered a good substitute, for, on the one hand, it is not immaterial to the developing countries whether resources are obtained through a negotiated loan or through a gift and, on the other, their liquidity problems remain pressing.

Chapter VI

STRUCTURAL PROBLEMS IN INTERNATIONAL MONETARY MANAGEMENT AND THEIR IMPLICATIONS FOR DEVELOPMENT FINANCE

by *Irving S. Friedman*

Introduction[1]

My personal concern with the international monetary system is a dual one, stemming from my own experience. Having been there, at the establishment of this system and spending the succeeding years closely involved with the problems of bilateral exchange control, exchange restrictions and how to achieve an international monetary system based on currency convertibility and internationally agreed par values, I view the establishment of convertibility and the continuing spirit of cooperation as the key stone of that system. My more recent involvement with development finance, has brought about greater, not lesser, concern with that system. For it plays a critical role in the economic lives of the world's developing nations: the adequacy, terms, and directions of the flow of development finance, aimed to enable these nations to grow into viable participants in the international monetary system, are themselves dependent on the maintenance of an effective international monetary system and the solution of underlying international economic prolbems.

An international monetary system will work, and work well, if all nations cooperate, adhering to the same set of "rules of the game", even if those rules were quite different from the present ones. The present "rules", largely incorporated in the Articles of Agreement of the Fund,

---

1. The author plans to expand these thoughts into a longer article. He wishes to acknowledge the assistance given to him in this work by Dr. E. Yudin. The views expressed are those of the author and not necessarily those of the World Bank.

reflect both a choice of adjectives and a choice of instruments to achieve those objectives. Cooperation itself requires a dual conviction on the part of the system's participants. Without the dual conviction that the system *can* satisfy requirements of individual nations and that individual nations *will*, in fact, act responsibly in accord with the established system, no system can function. Its participants will rely on escape clauses or, worse, ignore international commitments when those commitments conflict with national interests.

Clearly then, international rules must take account of known distinctions among national economies, and all that goes importantly into national policy making. The future stability of any international consensus may depend on the accumulation and systematic analysis of such knowledge which must, then, be realistically incorporated into that consensus.

To accomplish this, we need to know the real phenomena that underlie monetary data. Much of what we do know is, unfortunately, partial or exemplary rather than structural or systematic; and, to say the least, it lacks international comparability. I have long felt the conviction (and voiced it repeatedly on other occasions) that such key elements in the analysis of international monetary relationships have been accorded insufficient attention, magnifying the difficulties we face in attempting to achieve continuous and successful balance of payments management nationally and to develop avenues of collaboration and cooperation internationally.

Yet, cooperative arrangements, particularly since the late 1950's—for example, the increases in International Monetary Fund quotas, the creation and use of swap agreements and the General Agreements to Borrow, the regular meetings in Basle and those in Washington to design the two-tier gold market and in Stockholm to formalize the Special Drawing Rights proposal, the establishment and deliberations of Working Party III of the OECD—have played important parts in maintaining the viability of the international monetary system. These have given the system greater flexibility in dealing with non-monetary as well as monetary phenomena. Although the provision of liquidity has been the primary focus of these arrangements, real factors in the adjustment process are being given increasing attention. What I will stress, therefore, differs essentially in degree, but there is much to be gained from even greater attention to real phenomena and failure to do so may well jeopardize the effective functioning of the international monetary system. Our concern must lie with both supplies of liquidity and the effects of real phenomena. For neither is, in fact, independent of the other.

I regard the concept of international monetary cooperation, its acceptance and implementation as one of the major forward steps of our generation. Hence, I will not deal here with the deficiencies of the system from the perspective of encouraging disenchantment with that concept. Instead, I will focus on what we can do to effect improvement. I will consider, first, some of the ways in which the prevailing modes of balance of payments analysis fail to embrace broad structural, political and social considerations. From that discussion, I then draw some conclusions both for national and international policies.

We have, at present, had enough experience to hope that the deficiencies can both be recognized and overcome. We can, then, lay the groundwork for ever closer approximation to those goals in the future.

Neglected factors

The analysis of balance of payments problems and policies have been typically discussed within a broad Keynesian framework and, more specifically, within the monetary portions of that construct. This limited perspective cannot, by itself, answer the questions that arise in every day policy making.

What questions should we be addressing? They fall, broadly, into three groups. First, *what are the key elements* in national economies and in international economic relations which affect nations' balance of payments and, thereby, influence international monetary relations and the functioning and management of the international monetary system? Second, *are these elements being given adequate attention* either in national policy making, particularly in the nation's management of its balance of payments, or in international deliberations on the functioning of the international monetary system? Or, do key questions suffer virtually systematic neglect? And, finally, where attention is inadequate, *how do we remedy that neglect?*

Without denying relevance to the building blocks of the Keynesian model—the consumption function, investment demand, liquidity preference—I suggest that critical aspects of the answers to the first question lie within the given conditions of the general Keynesian framework. Keynesian analysis is itself essentially short-term, formulated in real terms with the pattern and level of productive capacity, like the availability of technology, treated as given conditions. It tends to presume that all transactions, national and international, have commercial origins. It retains the classical assumption that monetary phenomena will predictably, directly and automatically reflect any real changes.

Having said only this much, recall how frequently in studying specific problems we modify these same assumptions. Each of us recognizes that any single monetary observation reflects the net impact of a complex composite of real events. Those events, we know, may incorporate things like on-going structural changes; many may, moreover, be political or social, not commercial in origin. Neither would any of us deny the existence of real change in the long-run, or that these changes must, inter alia, have impacts on a country's balance of payments. Furthermore, it seems obvious that two countries experiencing simultaneous but dissimilar real adjustments will likewise evince not only different balance of payments behavior but different problems of efficient management of the balance of payments.

Yet, remaining subsumed within given conditions, it is a fact that these factors often suffer inadequate attention, if not widespread neglect in general academic discussion of monetary policy or international monetary relations. The level of attention is inadequate when it means that we treat relevant questions as inconsequential ones; it is negligent when we fail even to see such questions. The impact of international differences in patterns of structural change on international monetary relations are tempting to ignore; the questions they raise are most difficult to analyze and answer. Although prima facie glances at data reveal, if partially, how countries differ quantitatively, our framework may blind us to important ancillary questions: why do countries stay different? Or, to what extent are the economic forces underlying observed differences themselves influenced by national political or social conditions? And, can we specify the manner in which national conditions—political, social or structural—contrain the government's selection among available international policy options?

In treating all international financial transactions as though commercially motivated, we may put on another pair of blinders: we purchase foreign money to settle international debt. But none would query the contention noted by many that two distinct types of activity can give rise to that debt: first, commercial activity which depends on relative prices and, second, political activity which, if it reflects price considerations at all, reflects a quite different set of opportunity costs. The nation's foreign-exchange market position, like its balance of payments statement, illustrates the financial implication of *all* its global involvements—political and social as well as commercial. If we persist in treating all transactions as though commercially initiated, can we precisely evaluate the costs and benefits of a nation's balance of payments or exchange market position? Can we meaningfully identify fundamental disequilibrium? Or, are we able to measure progress toward mutually determined ends? Can we, for example, even quantify in any truly economic way the net resource flow to developing nations?

There is another, perhaps more critical, sense in which we allow the spectrum of our vision to diminish: we know that the public sector has expanded far beyond its minimal nineteenth century role and even beyond what Keynes specified. Governments now pursue a greater number of policy objectives than ever before; full employment with price stability has been added to traditional aims of internal and external balance. It is equally clear that government's investment decisions and its ability profoundly to effect income redistribution mean that it can and does, indeed, impinge on every sphere of economic and social activity.

The public sector is often so large that unless its potential power is contravened by vested interest groups or ideological impediments, it will be the most important element in affecting not only national policy, but international balance of payments management and international economic relations as well.

Available data do indicate major international variations in the absolute and relative size of public sectors' activities. We have yet, however, to attempt rigorous analysis of the national impact of such variations or to describe and compare internationally, past and present degrees of dependence among sectors of the economy. Neither have we fully comprehended the international impact of prevailing disparities in the public sector's power among nations; we have merely the general sense that the public sector has become much more important and that problems of resource mobilization and resource allocation within the public sector are among the primary factors in a country's economic behavior, nationally and internationally. But much more studying and thinking needs to be done as a basis for national policy making, including how to transform an economic understanding into practical politics.

Paralleling that national phenomenon, we observe (with somewhat fuller understanding) that nations themselves have become increasingly internationally interdependent. The post-war years have witnessed tremendous increases in international interdependence globally and regionally, an interdependence accompanied by increases in international governmental consultation and cooperation, both formal and informal. Because of the increasing importance of governmental decisions the international economic system is, in this sense, becoming smaller, not larger, with fewer critical decision makers, not more.

Greater interdependence is coupled with greater uncertainty, and the combination of these two characteristics suggests that relationships among nations in the international area bear more in common with those among competing firms in an oligopolistically, rather than a perfectly competitive market as some seem to assume.

As long as we continue to accord insufficient attention to the effects of increased interdependence and uncertainty in international relationships, to distinctions between commercial and other types of global involvement and, most important, to the impacts of real changes—structural, political or social—on nations' domestic and foreign policies and attitudes, we will continue to incur unnecessary costs resulting from reduced efficiency of the international monetary system. The costs of underestimating the importance of these factors are, if not greatest then most obvious to the developing nations.

In order to develop real resources, these countries need a consistent, large and rising flow of funds, especially for the public sector. If repeated crises augment uncertainty within the international monetary system they limit those flows and thereby impede economic development. The largest capital markets and the financial structures most appropriate for arranging international capital movements are located in the United States and the United Kingdom. Yet, their currencies have been afflicted by crises and both have limited capital flows to the developing countries to levels well below where they might otherwise be. Although Germany has become an important alternative source of development funds, her capital market and financial structure cannot, of course, substitute for the United States and the United Kingdom.

Budgetary pressures may further restrict the flow of public funds from the more advanced nations. Preoccupied with domestic needs, their officials view an excess of government expenditures over receipts as a potential stimulus to domestic inflation which must be eliminated. If the broader implications of development funds are imperfectly understood or ignored, items of assistance to the developing countries are easily excised.

While domestic budgetary pressures can limit public flows of development finance, conditions in the developed countries' capital markets can make private sources of development funds inaccessible or accessible only at prohibitively high financial costs. The developed nations correctly regard exchange rate change as an extreme measure: changes in their exchange rates have, therefore, been relatively infrequent. As a result, their authorities place greater reliance on interest rate shifts or fiscal policy for short-term balance of payments management. But fiscal policy is often inadequate, for example, expenditures are excessive in relation to receipts, or absorb an excessive proportion of total private savings, or create manpower bottlenecks, etc. Swift adjustment of fiscal policy is difficult technically, even when desired politically, and too often the political desire is too weak; monetary policy is left to assume the lion's share of these countries' short-term adjustment burden. It is not surprising, then, to find high interest rates and rather volatile capital markets in which patterns of funds' movements are unpredictable and even perverse. Under such circumstances, institutions in the developed countries become even more concerned with liquidity than they would be if the future availability of adequate savings were regarded with more confidence. This preoccupation with liquidity results in the closest scrutiny of each borrower's creditworthiness; risk-taking is even more discouraged than usual and, when done, demands a high financial return. All this makes the developing nations' access to private capital markets in the developed countries difficult, if not impossible.

But the financing of economic development and hence development itself depends in good measure on access to savings in the developed countries and thus on the good operation of the international monetary system. When things get tough or uncertain, developed countries have recourse to domestic finance, accumulated reserves and, possibly, foreign funds. Developing countries have few of these, and if monetary relations among developed nations are shaky, those sources of funds, public and private, evaporate. This is no small cost. Neither is their benefit from a more comprehensive approach to international monetary arrangements small: it could bring about the conditions necessary to evoke sustained and rising flows of funds from abroad. Without these funds, these countries cannot hope to develop economically, becoming viable participants in the international monetary system.

Yet, it must be noted that even ideal international monetary conditions would not guarantee a flow of funds. If the international monetary system determines the flow of funds supply schedule, conditions within the developing nations themselves determine the corresponding demand schedule. The two interact. Presumably, the supply of funds will flow elsewhere if recipients persistently utilize them inefficiently. Hence, the need for change allowing better economic resource utilization, like the benefits from a smooth flow of funds, is particularly dramatic in the developing nations. Resource utilization questions bring us deeply into the working of the real economy of these nations.

Remedies

What is required is the continued accumulation, coordination and analysis of knowledge of these real factors. For example, as much of our work within the Bank has shown, sectoral analyses of nation's balance of payments accounts may highlight existing inconsistencies between sectoral policy decisions and their implications for national economic policy, particularly (but not solely) with respect to the balance of payments. Knowledge of national economic structures and of national economic goals and priorities—even those beyond the economic sphere—is, then, a step toward understanding what a nation's balance of payments position or policy actually conveys about the national economy's international interaction.

A reflection of governments' inability or unwillingness to grapple with the deep-seated difficulties which disturb the system appears in the recent crises. The crises are symptomatic. Symptoms may subside. But as long as we lack full knowledge of the root-causes of the illness, new symptoms will appear or old ones recur with greater insistence. Wrong decisions, where the pathology is incomplete, can be dangerous ones.

The symptoms, here, are monetary but, as I argued above, we cannot diagnose the illness until we look into the real phenomena and seemingly intractable problems where the root-cause can be uncovered. We need a broader perspective, one which bases itself realistically on the international economy as it exists and operates today and on how it wants to function in the future. Only then should we consider changing the prescription; we will then be better diagnosticians.

As is apparent from what I have already said, greater wisdom and improved policy making require greater disaggregation of the national economy and international economic relations and, necessarily therefore, greater complexity. In practice, I envision an essentially iterative process involving successive stages of decision making; at each stage previous tentative decisions are reevaluated in the light of new information. Close and careful specification of national aims and practices, and like examination of national models, yields the first stage, tentative policy conclusions for the foreseeable future. At this stage, countries must select development strategies which take account of known interdependencies and incorporate the naturally accompanying uncertainties and differentials in balance of payments effects. They must, in that light, formulate tentative policies to achieve the objectives of those strategies.

Two sources of leadership in this task already exist within developing countries—planning commissions or their equivalent, usually headed by a Minister or, indeed at times by the Prime Minister, and central banks. Both agencies appropriately view the country as a totality, and should regard themselves as natural allies. Both should serve as politically autonomous technical authorities. Acting together, the central bank can lend the strong, independent weight of its support to the planning commission's priorities over and against vested interests and vice-versa. To do this, there is needed an evolution of a clear system of national priorities —by central banks on the monetary side, by planning commissions on the real side—formulated with the realization that growth and stability are two sides of the same coin.

International consultations are the second stage of the iterative process, providing the vehicle for reconciliation of the many national forecasts of the behavior of the real economy not only with one another but with accepted international aims and practices. Reconciliation may involve a third stage in the process: mutual modification both of the tentative conclusions and of internationally agreed arrangements. International services of this type must, then, design the machinery for reconciliation and adjustment. These are too important to be left to diverse national government policies or to mere chance. They need the rule of law.

The rule of law that does prevail in the area of international monetary relationships—the evolving international monetary system—was the quite natural outgrowth of central bank development and the evolution of relationships between the country's central bank and its Ministry of Finance or Treasury. Now the entire nation-state has taken key importance in the world of economic behaviour; we recognized during World War II the broad nature of international economic relations, spanning money trade, wealth and development. The lack of a rule of law in the other areas makes the monetary rule of law less effective. It fragments the economic world and forces the international monetary system to bear the brunt of the burden of cooperation. The evolutionary process which has brought about today's international monetary system should be preparing for the next step: a movement toward establishing a parallel system for real, as well as monetary economic relations.

There have been some attempts, if not at the formulation of rules of law, at least at analyses of real phenomena as they affect specific relationships. From the Marshall Plan, through NATO and the European Payments Union, in Point IV and in the Codes of Trade and Liberalization and of Payments, under the aegis of the OECD, the discussions of the adjustment process within the framework of Working Party III, the economic work of the World Bank, the broadening of the IMF's work and so on, many studies have begun to form interrelated pieces of this massive jigsaw puzzle. These at times have been quite comprehensive, but never complete. One vast missing area requiring closer agreement on international rules of conduct arises in that of development. The total design is itself far from finished; it sums to little more than a preliminary sketch, but there is a wealth of post-war experience that we have only begun to tap to provide a guide.

This is not a time for plans for the reform of the international economic system: plans will come forth if there is a market for them. We can specialize in our investigations and suggestions. It may be that specialized agencies can design appropriate rules, but only if they coordinate in the application of such rules. We will otherwise find ourselves again in a situation not very different from our present one. There is, in consequence, a need for international synthesis, for political decisions on the highest level.

It is the same need for coordination between monetary and planning authorities that exists nationally. The international counterpart of such coordination lies in closer cooperation between the International Monetary Fund and the World Bank. Both institutions have at least begun to recognize this. The Fund takes a broad approach to the monetary issues it faces; the Bank examines real economic factors, but not in isolation from the impact of monetary changes. A counterpart for Europe would evolve with a further extension of multilateral surveillance to a more detailed analysis of the entire economy, real as well as monetary, and with greater integration of the analyses of real phenomena.

We are, fortunately, well ahead of the 1940's. Our experience and understanding stand us in good stead; the machinery for international consultation and collaboration in our fields—the IMF, the World Bank, the BIS, the regional banks, and so forth—already exist. And they have been tried and found successful. What we need is to analyze the tough questions involved in evaluating the complex interrelations of real and monetary phenomena, nationally and internationally, and to arrive at practical answers. In this way we will be laying the basis both for a better management and operation of the international monetary system and a more adequate flow of needed capital to the developing countries.

Chapter VII

THE SOCIALIST COUNTRIES AND THE INTERNATIONAL MONETARY SYSTEM

by *L. Veltruský* and *J. Petrivalský*

Introduction

Two basic facts from the post-war history of international monetary co-operation may have influenced the socialist countries' approach to this problem:

a. The transition to a developed international monetary system took a considerably longer time than had been initially estimated. In addition, the system proposed by the Bretton Woods conception did not come generally, into existence in a direct way, but a number of countries reached it through certain interim forms of monetary co-operation. This circuitous route seems to have been caused not only by economic but in some cases by political considerations as well.

b. The present system of international monetary co-operation has been facing a number of new problems involving constant discussion of its reform. This seems to be quite adequate and will probably continue with changing and developing economic conditions.

One might also cite here certain serious descrepancies which disrupt the harmonious functioning of the international monetary system. Mr. Alain Cedel, in his article "Le Système monétaire international de 1929 à 1968" (*L'Economie*, Oct. 1, 1968) mentioned, e.g. the contradiction between the statutory equality of each currency and the factual non-convertibility of a number of national currencies;

the contradiction between the specific needs of the countries of the third world and the right to a quota-bound volume of credit,[1] in other

---

1. According to the Articles of Agreement of the IMF.

words, the contradiction between the possibilities of members privileged by their economic standing and those of economically less-developed members;

the contradiction between the advantages for the two countries that issue reserve currencies and the fact that these advantages can be achieved only since the other states surrender part of their national sovereignty;[2]

the contradiction arising from the fact that reserve currencies can provide international liquidity only if their issue exceeds the national needs of a given country; under certain circumstances this weakens the international position of the currency concerned. Further, one might mention the close links between the currency and gold, the freezing of the price of gold and the limited inflow of monetary gold.

These factors and contradictions cannot be overlooked in considering the relation between the socialist countries and the IMF.

For the socialist countries the situation is even more complicated. Important aspects include the political situation and the general development of Comecon countries. Nor can it be overlooked that a system of clearing-payments does exist among the Comecon countries, closely linked to the methods of management of their internal economies.[3] Further, there still do exist certain differences in the level of economic development reached by individual countries.

One of the basic general problems of the international monetary system is to encourage the countries still outside it to participate more intensively in the international division of labour. Approach to the international division of labour remains a basic question. There cannot even

---

2. This limitation of national sovereignty has various aspects, including fixing and changing exchange rates, not converting the dollar or sterling holdings into gold, etc.
3. In general, clearing agreements are bound to the bilateral trade agreements. Agreements for the exchange of goods form a part of the planned tasks of enterprises or a part of planned deliveries to the enterprises. In most countries special foreign trade firms deal as exclusive mediators. Within the framework of this system the clearing payments remain practically bilateral unless the use of a surplus of country A towards country B to cover a deficit towards country C is facilitated by respective trade agreements or delivery protocols.

be any consideration of co-operation with an international monetary system as long as the economic necessity of opening up an economy is not felt and the basic prerequisites for this are not established and as long as some countries continue to see advantages in a closed economy. The problem of a closed or open economy is not a clearcut one in the present economic situation and specific position of each country, even though, in the long-term view, autarchic tendencies lead to backwardness.

From the point of view of short-term interests, international competition entails numerous disadvantages and dangers. The country's needs have to be taken in longer perspective. This can occur only if a country has reached a relatively high level of economic development. For economically strong and developed countries the liberalisation of trade and of payments does not entail doubts or economic hesitation. Here we are dealing with economic aspects, which can, needless to say, be greatly influenced by political events, and vice versa.

Developments in the socialist countries and relations with IMF

Closer contacts between the socialist countries and the international monetary system present, in theory and practice, a very complex problem, involving not only economic but also political matters. If we are concerned with the future of the international monetary system, it should be said that inside the Comecon system there also exists a great deal of discussion as to the future of its monetary system.

Comecon member states constantly criticize the insufficient intensity and efficiency of their mutual division of labour and the low share of Comecon countries in world trade. While their share in world industrial output amounts to over 30 per cent of the total, their share in world trade makes up only approximately 10 per cent.

The decisive factor for the establishment of Comecon has probably not been the objective pressure of international economic relations within the socialist countries, but speedy industrialisation and strenghtening of defence potential, the transformation of agriculture and changes in the standard of living. Economic growth was mainly tied to extensive factors. Exaggerated stress was placed on economic independence. The effects of embargo policy applied by Western countries in the period of the cold war should not however be underestimated. A number of Comecon member states were in the early fifties among countries with a low proportion of industry to agriculture. (Bulgaria, for example, had 25 : 75, Roumania 39 : 61, Hungary 32 : 58, Poland 47 : 53). Today this proportion of industrial to agricultural production in the European Comecon countries has changed and amounts to roughly 70 : 30%, and the support of agriculture is among present problems.

The main feature of the economic reform in the socialist countries is to raise the efficiency of the economy. This would require a more intense and more flexible economic co-operation between socialist countries, which would stimulate integrating processes within Comecon. The rate of growth in trade among Comecon countries has, however, been far lower up to now than the growth rate of trade between the developed western countries. Criticism has been advanced with regard to the isolation of the internal economies of Comecon countries from external markets, the neglecting of commercial principles in foreign trade, the disintegration of multilateral relations into bilateral ones, the limitation and inflexibility of international monetary relations. Hence the future relations of the socialist countries with the international monetary system depend on possible variants of developments in the socialist countries and on the expected and necessary changes in the international monetary system. In our paper we wish to deal primarily with the former problem.

The very mechanism of monetary co-operation causes specific problems in developed countries, in developing countries and in the socialist countries.

The economic system of the socialist countries is undergoing a number of reforms at the present time. Under the "classic" administrative and directive system of planning, co-operation with the IMF was hardly conceivable. Passively, it was exposed to the pressure of world development. The economic changes inside Comecon might lead to greater integration within this area and growing isolation from the rest of the world.

But they equally well might lead to a more active approach to the world-wide division of labour, together with widening economic cooperation inside the Comecon countries.

Historical experiences reveal that as long as—in general—international economic relations develop on the basis of integration within a certain block, discriminatory trends between this block and the economies of other countries or blocks will grow stronger. It would seem that this occurs even when, from the onset, the final aim is alleged to be international division of labour on a world-wide scale.

Contradictions within the systems can prevent co-operation between them, but can also act as a stimulus for such co-operation. If we assume that changes will take place within the blocks, the question arises which system adopted by the IMF will be more attractive and will ease the participation of Comecon countries in international monetary co-operation. In this regard it will be important whether the international monetary system returns to the rigid forms of the gold standard or whether the broadening of international liquidity develops in flexible forms (e.g. credit facilities).

Possible relations with IMF

In considering the future development of relations between the IMF and the socialist countries we must take into account the different variants and combinations, since even from the viewpoint of future Comecon monetary systems there exist different currents of thought, some with a real chance of being implemented.

For the sake of completeness mention should also be made of certain variants that tend to be rather of a theoretical and model character.

Development inside Comecon might theoretically assume any of these forms (one possibility, i.e. direct relations between Comecon institutions and the international monetary system, being left aside):

—accession of individual socialist countries to the IMF, with simultaneous changes of the monetary system within Comecon;

—accession of a group of Comecon countries to the IMF, which presupposes that inside Comecon a certain differentiation in the development of the monetary system takes place in such a way that a group of countries with more intense economic pressure towards internationalisation will be formed.

It remains problematic in both cases whether a certain degree of convertibility for non-residents would be achieved. With broad economic relations among Comecon countries the convertibility of a certain currency for non-residents would probably mean that a country with non-convertible currency would cover its imports from Western countries by exports to the country that has introduced convertibility for non-residents. If—this is a further variant—two monetary systems were to come into being, and with them two spheres of international economic relations, i.e. if a certain country were to introduce convertibility only towards areas with convertible currencies and keep the system of clearing payments for its relations to countries with non-convertible currencies, the disintegration of the monetary unit within the country would continue.

Such a disintegration is the reason for the existence of a number of internal exchange rates, which would be simply a repetition of the current situation. More likely, therefore, is some form of co-operation of the whole Comecon area with simultaneous changes in the monetary system inside the area towards multilaterality of the payments system and the establishment of conditions for the general transferability of the leading national currency or for that of a special conventional money unit.

Such an approach would presuppose the rapid abandonment of autarchic trends, which occur the varying extents in different Comecon countries. The different degree of technical standards in production, however, encourages protectionism and autarchic trends, even though, in the long-term perspective, these trends simultaneously act as features conserving backwardness.

At the present time only Yugoslavia is a member of the IMF. Some of the present Comecon members have belonged to the IMF in the past.

It is very likely that in all socialist countries there exist concrete ideas for possible relations with the IMF and for the future of the entire monetary system. But with a view to economic and political factors it can hardly be assumed that each Comecon country will solve the matter of co-operation with the IMF, separately or without mutual consultations. There exist political factors and logical fears that isolated moves of individual countries towards such co-operation would weaken trends towards co-operation within Comecon. Factors to be taken into account include these:

a. Trade between socialist countries represents a predominant part of the overall foreign trade of these countries;

b. The Comecon countries are closely linked through the existing mechanism of economic co-operation;

c. Some products of Comecon countries are not fully competitive, for their exports are oriented to relatively soft markets;

d. Some Comecon countries differ in their level of development and have not yet achieved a higher degree of industrialization.

Assuming that the system of economic, political and military blocks continues for some time to come, it is hardly likely that the Comecon countries will adopt separate standpoints towards the future of the international monetary system or that they would individually take steps in that direction.

We therefore consider it decisive in discussing co-operation between the socialist countries and the international monetary system that account should be taken of the main variants of future monetary co-operation among the Comecon countries themselves.

Variants of monetary cooperation among Comecon countries

The following variants would seem most important:

a. The existing systems of payments among Comecon countries will continue (with certain minor adjustments). This is based on the clearing system bound with the bilateral trade agreements and using the Clearing Rouble and the International Bank for Economic Co-operation (Comecon Bank).

b. By the side of the clearing system of payments in transferable Roubles in its present form there will come into being payment in the national currencies of the Comecon countries, with growing features of liberalisation of foreign trade.

c. A transferable currency will be introduced for all the Comecon countries.

The Comecon Bank was founded in 1963. Transferable Roubles began to be used in 1964. The establishment of the Comecon Bank and the introduction of this transferable Rouble was to help to overcome bilateral trade relations and replace the Clearing Rouble used up to that time.

The turnover of trade between Comecon countries grew considerably in the years 1965-1968 and at the same time the volume of trade outside Comecon expanded.

The growth of payments relations between socialist countries was primarily of a quantitative character, connected with the growth of mutual trade. From a qualitative viewpoint the function of the transferable Rouble did not bring any great changes. In essence, the transferable Rouble is a clearing unit with strong elements of bilaterality because the system of bilateral trade relations has remained unchanged. In considering the development of monetary relations, we must bear in mind the decisive role of trends towards the strenghtening of factors of value.

The present payments system among Comecon Bank members is influenced by further specific conditions.

Among the more important are:

a. The prompt manner of payment for deliveries.

b. The use of long-term contract prices.

c. Considerable limitation for the direct participation of manufacturing firms in foreign trade.

d. Various ways in different countries of balancing differences between contract prices and internal wholesale prices out of, or to the benefit of the state budget. This separation of the internal price level from the external price structure even within Comecon has led to multiple exchange rates, each differing from the official rate of exchange.

From the standpoint of relations between Comecon countries and

Comecon Bank members there exist certain discrepancies in their approach to the international monetary system.

The socialist countries are greatly interested in expanding trade with western countries and in a relatively stable world monetary system. A number of circumstances, however, has led to a clearing system of payments which—under the conditions in which it works—is isolated from the world monetary system. Unless the current clearing payments between socialist countries change basically, the possibilities of active co-operation between the two systems probably remain rather limited.

But economic reality proves that closed systems cause quite exceptional difficulties for technical development and, at the present time, represent one of the most serious obstacles to economic progress as such. On the other hand, the socialist countries with strong, steadily growing production capacity, relatively highly qualified labour and the possibility of reaching world standard in a number of products relatively soon, constitute a large market for the Western countries. The isolation of this market would in itself negate the optimal conditions for world economic development. So it would seem that on both sides there are clear points of interests in speeding up the development of mutual economic relations.

The possibility therefore exists that, given favourable conditions, closer co-operation between the Comecon countries and the IMF, might come into being, contributing towards the stabilisation of the international monetary system.

At the present time, the Comecon Bank's trade in gold and convertible currencies is increasing. The reserves of monetary gold and foreign assets in convertible currencies and the volume of trade in these currencies is, however, very small. But it can be assumed that this type of trade will gradually expand.

A further alternative in the development of payments systems between Comecon Bank members is payment in national currencies. Proposals to this effect have been put forward by Czechoslovak economists, who suggest that a third sphere should be created by the side of the existing clearing payments in transferable Roubles, i.e. payments in national currencies. Certain circumstances justify the temporary continuation of the clearing system.

It is assumed that the clearing payments sphere would be largely limited to present forms of economic co-operation (contract prices, prompt methods of payment, non-convertibility, etc.), whereas payment in national currencies would involve the liberalisation of foreign trade, with more flexible organisational forms, market prices mutual convertibility of national currencies among participating countries, active participation of manufacturing and trading firms, the expansion of services, foreign trade credits, and the like.

Such a change presents difficult problems both from the economic and political point of view. It could be nevertheless expected that the suggestions of certain Comecon countries for more flexible mutual trade and its partial liberalisation will be supported by the ruling political circles of these countries. In such a case the monetary co-operation between socialist countries and the world monetary system would broaden for a partial liberalisation of foreign trade would ensue. The partial convertibility of the national currencies of the socialist countries would require the existence of a reserve currency for adjustment of deficits in the balance of payments in this mutually liberalised trade.

This purpose might be served by some convertible western currency, though this would cause many problems, or by some new, perhaps conventional convertible money unit.

This form of development would lead to basic changes in the very monetary basis of relations between Comecon Bank members and the world monetary system.

In recent months certain proposals have been put forward aimed at the establishment of a transferable currency, i.e. one that could be freely used within the framework of the Comecon Bank. However, the ways proposed to achieve this aim differ.

It might be said that there exist two basic propositions:

a. a universal one, and

b. a partial one.

The universal solution takes its starting point in the fact that the system of economic co-operation of Comecon countries is no longer suited to the conditions of developing trade, that this trade is lagging behing the rate of production. It is believed that, within a short period, all participating countries will become interested in the liberalisation of foreign trade in all main directions. As proof, the economic reforms at present taking place in the majority of socialist countries are pointed to. The liberalisation of foreign trade would change the position of manufacturing and trading enterprises, the prices at which the socialist countries are trading and the conditions of payments, and would furthermore provide prerequisites for multilaterality and herewith for a transferable currency.

To prevent the economic co-operation of Comecon countries from developing in isolation from western markets this transferable currency would be partially convertible for gold or for convertible currencies.

It is, at rock-bottom, a universal solution, which would encompass all countries and all monetary and commodity aspects of transferability (and, at a later stage, even transferability of capital).

The implementation of this variant would greatly encourage co-operation between the socialist countries and the world monetary system.

It would greatly strengthen interest in the stabilisation of the international monetary system and in conditions for the more flexible creation of international liquidity, and in overcoming problems ensuing from narrow ties between international liquidity and national currencies.

The implementation of this variant is highly unlikely at the present time, for a number of reasons. Consequently, some countries are beginning to stress the partial solution. This assumes that the present state of payments in transferable Roubles can be overcome only by stages. One way out would be to set up a third Rouble sphere, i.e. to assume that, apart from the Soviet and the transferable Rouble, there would exist a sphere of payments in convertible Roubles. The idea comprising several proposals, is based on two main principles:

a. Part of the trade between Comecon countries in the field of mass-produced consumer goods would be liberalised.

b. Surpluses in this liberalised foreign trade would be accumulated in

Roubles, which would be convertible for gold or convertible currencies.

The partial solution would, of course, be of very limited effect, both for the narrow sphere of commodities and since the convertibility of assets for gold could, under present conditions, strengthen bilaterality to avoid the possibility of asking the debts of a country to be paid in convertible currencies or in gold.

Participation of the socialist countries in the international monetary system

These variants show that the active participation of the socialist countries in the international monetary system encounters great difficulties for economic reasons. Yet the decisive factor in any decision must be sought in political developments, especially in agreement between the two Super-Powers. The creation of a favourable political climate would, in all likelihood, ease the spread of East-West trade, and would have a favourable effect on trade even between socialist countries, on its liberalisation and flexibility and the ensuing development of monetary-co-operation. We base ourselves on the assumption that by 1975 the monetary problems among the Comecon countries will find a partial solution either through partial convertibility of national currencies or the creation of a common monetary unit for Comecon countries convertible for gold or convertible currencies. Further, that monetary co-operation between the socialist countries will be based on fixed exchange rates unified for current payments. The question of links between the national currencies of socialist countries of the new Comecon supra-national monetary unit and gold or convertible currencies as well as the question of fixed exchange rates is closely bound up with the further development of the world monetary system.

The latter is a highly complex question. It is not our place to propose new ideas. Nevertheless, attention might be drawn to certain specific aspects of the questions under discussion in this book. There is perhaps no need to emphasize that what we are saying is our personal point of view, which does not necessarily coincide with the opinions of other men of theory and practice.

In our opinion it would be useful to mention the problems of: the demonetisation of gold; the flexibility of exchange rates; the creation of international liquidity through credit facilities and the movement of international capital.

We do not intend to investigate these problems as such, only to make a few comments from our standpoint.

In suggesting variants of possible monetary development among Comecon countries we mentioned that is likely that the countries would adopt gold for their mutual payments system (either directly or indirectly). This seems to suggest that it would appear generally useful for currencies to be based on the gold standard. It might easily be assumed that the authors of this chapter hold a similar view as to the world monetary system. This, in fact, is not the case.

In our view, the Comecon and world monetary systems will continue to develop differently for some time to come. In view of the conditions prevailing within Comecon it is useful for that system to be directly or indirectly supported by the gold base, whereas, on a world scale, measures should be taken towards the demonetisation of gold. From the socialist countries' viewpoint such a step would create better general prerequisites for the establishment of a controlled world monetary system. Theoretically, worldwide controlled currency suits planned economies better. But we assume that political and economic conditions will make possible a collective, truly world-wide control of the monetary system. In theory, it might, therefore, be assumed that in future international payment relations gold will be replaced in proportion as conditions for a controlled world currency improve. So far, gold facilitates the functioning of the world monetary system under conditions where there is a lack of trust in the relative economic stability of individual countries or blocks. This lack of trust results probably from these countries or blocks being conceived as more or less isolated and since international economic co-operation is not yet sufficiently strong to overcome this isolation. On the other hand, within the national economies the concept of monetary relations to gold as a guarantee of internal monetary and economic stability has already been overcome.

Even though gold as a link for the world-wide monetary system can still pay a positive role, it will not, in the immediate future, be able to do so quantitatively. This has given rise to the hypothesis that all countries in the world, insofar as they are interested in optimal economic development, will likewise be interested in forming an international monetary system, which should have sufficient stability owing to the agreement and the interest of all participants. Such a demand for economic rationality could assume dynamic force.

Views on the development of a world-wide monetary system

Any thoughts on the further development and setup of a world-wide monetary system must take into account a broad exchange of views on the advantages and disadvantages of fixed or fluctuating exchange rates. Without wishing to evaluate existing views in detail, it might be useful for us to state our views briefly.

Our starting point is that, under contemporary conditions, the exchange rate is not solely formed under the influence of supply and demand. The search for a rational influence over the growth of the national economy requires intervention in exchange rates, either directly by central monetary authorities on the exchange markets or through indirect tools of foreign trade policy, customs and fiscal policy. We are convinced that the system of fluctuating exchange rates would produce greater lability in the balance of payments, which would introduce even greater uncertainty into international trade and credit and payments relations, and be an obstacle rather than encouragement to international co-operation.

Advantageous for such co-operation can be considered those ideas that see a way to overcoming present shortcomings in the system of fixed exchange rates by widening the margins of their oscillations. Fixed rates of exchange with widened margins of oscillation would more quickly reflect differences in internal price levels and the purchasing power of national currencies in the exchange rate, would set free part of the existing exchange reserves and would act as an element of considerable stability, needed for future world-wide economic and monetary co-operation.

If we regard the future of the international monetary system from this point of view, the conviction grows that an international monetary system founded on fixed exchange rates and with widened margins of oscillation would create more favourable ground for the ultimate accession of the socialist countries to this system, even though we cannot exclude the possibility that some socialist countries will not be able to avoid fluctuating exchange rates for a certain period as they approach the true exchange rate.

Some theoreticians take a critical view of the road taken by the world monetary system at Bretton Woods. They are of the opinion that the creation of considerable international liquidity on the basis of reserve currencies is the cause of the present crisis of the system.

Others point to Keynes' well-known view of the need for the reorganisation of the world monetary system to be based not on the gold standard but on international credit money, and they have worked out variants of this original concept. We do not claim to be judges of the basic points of this dispute, but we would like to say that, in our personal view, (*a*) variants including such a supra-national conventional unit are a matter for the future; (*b*) The Comecon countries, in all likelihood, will take the road of parital convertibility of national currencies, with possibly the full convertibility of the leading currency of the block, and will, therefore, soon face certain problems similar to those in the western countries in the fifties.

Here lies, in our view, the difference between the Comecon countries and the world at large. While the Comecon monetary block will, in the near future, have to solve matters of convertibility of national currencies and the reserve currency of socialist countries, the world monetary system should evolve by separating international liquidity from reserve currencies.

This would give the world monetary system a certain flexibility. If it were to reach a stagnant point, stress would be laid on the gold standard and the aspect of national currencies as part of international liquidity. This would complicate the Comecon countries' accession to the world system, particularly in regard to the different level of their economies. We therefore believe that the present-day creation of international liquidity, viewed from the needs of the socialist countries, should become more flexible, both with the help of the SDR's and in other ways e.g. monetary co-operation of Central banks (i.e. swap operations).

The Bretton Woods Agreements were based on the development of the international monetary system and the organised international movement of capital. The latter might become an important factor in the liberalisation of foreign trade and closer monetary co-operation. We believe that these facts should be taken into consideration in discussing the problems of the Comecon countries. Some countries would be aided by the inflow of foreign capital, which would help advance the necessary changes in their economy, with a view to the liberalisation of foreign trade, the stabilisation of the exchange rate of the currency, and measures needed to make it convertible.

Chapter VIII

THE FUTURE OF THE
INTERNATIONAL MONETARY SYSTEM:
SUMMARY AND CONCLUSIONS

by *Paul Bareau*

The international monetary system, the outlines of which were drawn at Bretton Woods in 1944 and which has served the world since the end of World War II has been showing signs of strain. This should be said without derogation to a system which was conceived in an act of supreme economic foresight and statesmanship and which has served the world well. How well, may be measured by comparing the economic growth of member countries of the IMF and the expansion of world trade over the past 23 years with the monetary chaos and economic recession that marked much of the inter-war period.

The evidence of strain is to be found in the substantial and persistent imbalances that have developed in the balances of payments of some major countries. These, however, can be attributed more to inadequate policies on the part of individual countries concerned, than to inadequacies in the system.

The deficit in the US balance of payments may have persisted too long; but it must not be ignored that much of it reflected the aid given since the end of the war to other countries—not least those of Western Europe. This deficit helped the rebuilding of other countries' reserves and due tribute should be paid to what in some discussions is deemed to be a point of criticism.

There is, however, a two fold imbalance in the present international monetary system, firstly an obvious lack of equilibrium in the balances of payments of major countries and, secondly, a likely inadequacy of international reserves.

The US, the UK and France combined need an improvement of at least $ 7 to $ 8 billion in their balance of payments. Not more than half of this can be provided from the major current creditor countries, Germany, Italy and Japan. Hence a considerable increase in total world reserves will be needed to achieve the necessary solution of the present problem of imbalance.

Gold will not in present circumstances provide the required accretion of reserves. The bulk of the increase in reserves in recent years has been in foreign exchange holdings but a substantial proportion of this has been manufactured through swap transactions and cannot claim to have any permanence.

As is pointed out in chapter II: "The growth of global reserves has come to depend on there being payments difficulties somewhere in the system". The disequilibrium has been met partly by direct controls on exchange transactions and by restrictions which have been applied by surplus as well as deficit countries.

The growth of reserves must, therefore, depend on assets other than foreign currencies namely, gold, or gold equivalents.

On the role and price of gold, the majority opinion is that gold should remain a major and for a time the dominant element in international reserves but that its monetary price should remain unchanged at $ 35 per ounce. A few experts favour a substantial increase in the price but this is judged by the majority to be a regressive method of increasing world reserves and one which would distribute its immediate favours unfairly. It would, moreover, be contrary to the long, historical trend in the evolution of money, namely from "commodity moneys" to "credit moneys". This latter evolution had in recent years been accompanied by an unusually rapid erosion in the value of monies and this danger must be kept in mind in any attempt to create a new international fiduciary currency. This new element in international monetary reserves will be provided by the IMF Special Drawing Rights.

Criteria for reserve creation

If gold is to remain a relatively static, though still major element in reserves and if the amount held in the form of reserve currencies is now at or near its peak, the dynamic component of reserves must be provided by Special Drawing Rights operated through the IMF.

Ratification of the necessary amendments in the IMF Articles of Agreement by member countries should be completed this year but it is unlikely that the first activation of SDR's can be made before 1970.

In considering the criteria for assessing what is the appropriate creation of reserves it should be borne in mind that in the short run it is not the inadequacy of reserves that is responsible for the defects in the international monetary system. Defects of policy and not shortage of reserves have been the main culprit.

In some countries even negative reserves have failed to exercise the required discipline and restore balance of payments equilibrium. In others abundant and persistently rising reserves have taken a long time percolate into monetary and fiscal policies or lead to appropriate exports of capital.

In the long run, however, there has been and will continue to be a link between the amount of reserves and world economic expansion and trade. The decisions concerning the rate at which SDR's will be created should, therefore, be based on these longer term considerations and provide for issues over periods of five years.

The connection between the growth of world trade and that of world reserves is not a direct one since trade is financed by commercial bank credits and not out of reserves. The relation none the less exists because the larger the value of world trade the greater the likely oscillations in balances of payments which *are* financed from reserves. The same argument applies to movements of capital. The maximisation of productive and desirable international investment will be helped if there are reserves adequate to meet the resultant impact on the balances of payments of the capital exporting countries.

In discussions of the desirable rate of reserve creation there are dif-

ferences of views between those favouring a generous initial issue of
SDR's—say $ 4 billion—and those who feel that the credibility and
ready acceptance of this new type of reserve asset would be helped by a
more modest initial issue.

The "expansionists" argue that while the total reserves should continue to expand at about the same rate as in recent years—say by $2\frac{1}{2}$ per-
cent per annum—there should be an initial bonus issue. This would be
designed to make good the destruction of reserves induced by the repay-
ment of the swap facilities and other short and medium term credits
granted for exchange support operations.

If the present deficit countries are to switch into surplus, reconstitute
their depleted reserves and repay short term external debts, this will
cause considerable pressure on the reserves of other countries. To meet
this swing in balances of payments and the cancellation of reserves now
represented by IMF and intercentral Bank credits a generous initial
creation of SDR's is indicated.

The more cautious view is that the effectiveness of created reserves
depends on equal confidence in the various component reserve elements.

This has been advanced as one of the reasons for not being generous in
the initial issue of SDR's. Another reason is that countries must not
appear to be discouraged from pursuing sound economic policies and
encouraged to persist in balance of payments deficit.

It is generally agreed that the success of the SDR scheme depends on
the effectiveness of the mechanism for maintaining reasonable equilibrium in international balances of payments. The adjustment process is an
essential part of a system of created reserves. If this system is seen to be
merely another means of financing persistent deficits by some countries
the SDR scheme will have proved abortive.

Chapter IV gives the correct guidelines for the appropriate increase in
aggregate reserves. It should be "sufficient to provide countries with the
means of financing deficits while they take corrective measures to restore
their payments position without relying on deflation or trade and exchange restrictions. On the other hand the growth of reserves should not
be so plentiful or in such form, e.g. dollars, as to encourage countries

to delay unduly the adjustment of their balance of payments."

As, so often happens, the difficulty is to translate these impeccable principles into figures. What cannot be denied is that the creation of new reserves must be made on the confident assumption that the adjustment process will succeed. Some support the view that activation of the SDR scheme should not begin until there is real evidence that the required adjustments are seen to be taking place.

The adjustment process

The adjustment process is not only a matter of international consultation and of the system of multilateral surveillance which has been developed by OECD countries, but of national policy decisions with a large and in many cases dominantly political context.

Machinery for consultation exists in profusion including the Group of Ten, Working Party 3 of the OECD, the BIS and the IMF. But no international organisation has supranational authority to initiate decisions for adjustment purposes. A widespread view is that the system has done valuable work, in particular, by informing other countries of policy decisions projected or already made. This probably helps to explain why the international monetary system has weathered so many recent storms and why the imposition of exchange restrictions has led to so little retaliation.

But without decrying the machinery that has been established it must be admitted that it had had little direct identifiable influence on the policy decision of member countries. Its role must, in present circumstances, remain that of a father confessor and not a policeman.

In discussions of the adjustment mechanism and of its evident deficiencies it is agreed that the process must be of two-way character: that the obligations it places on deficit countries i.e. a mix of appropriate fiscal, monetary and incomes policy measures, should be matched by contrasting expansionist policies on the part of the surplus countries. Some opposition is voiced to the argument that surplus countries should be prepared, to inflate in order to do their duty in the adjustment process, but the suggestion can be made that a modest rise in prices of—say $1\frac{1}{2}$ per cent per annum—, would do them no harm and might do the two-way adjustment process some good. A considerable onus of adjustment must lie with the deficit countries though there should be a limit to the degree of deflation they are called upon to undergo. If this lies beyond their power or will, the process must be achieved by the appropriate devaluation of the currency. It should be added that an alternative to an unnecessary degree of "corrective" inflation in the surplus countries would be an upvaluation of their currencies.

Flexible rates

Should the process of adjustment aim at preserving fixed exchange parities, or should more flexible rates form a recognised and more widely used part of the adjustment mechanism?

This issue of flexible rates is the subject of much debate and widely conflicting views. There is no support for the claim that rates should be allowed to float freely. A flexible rate system could not be a substitute for good domestic internal adjustment policies. The damage this would cause to international trade and investment would be considerable. Moreover by encouraging speculative movements of funds greater flexibility of exchanges could "overkill" the adjustment process and thus lead to more and not less instability.

It could nevertheless be pointed out that the Bretton Woods system makes provision for rather more frequent changes of parities than have in fact taken place. The IMF might therefore be prepared to take confidential initiatives in suggesting exchange rate adjustments to its members and not wait for the member to make the application—which is often done too late and in conditions of crisis.

Various methods of introducing greater flexibility in exchange rates are being discussed: wider bands of permissible fluctuations around the fixed parities and adjustable pegs.

A number of practical difficulties could be seen in schemes of this kind. Against the proposal for a self-adjusting exchange rate mechanism it can be argued that exchange rate adjustment should always be a matter of policy choice, depending on diagnosis of a country's underlying position, and should not be determined by short term market trends.

The so-called "fork" proposal, under which countries should consult with the IMF whenever their reserves rise to an abnormally high level as well as when they fall to an excessively low level was discussed. In the absence of agreement about appropriate remedial policies, limitations could be placed on a country's right to continue to add to, or drawn on, its reserves to prevent any appreciation ordepre ciation of its exchange-rate.

Harmonisation of reserves

Unless the problem of harmonisation or equivalence of the various components in reserve assets is solved it could introduce an element of instability caused by some countries' preference for gold. That preference is now inhibited by voluntary arrangements not to convert dollars into gold. There are other ways in which some progress has already been made to preserve the existing proportions between reserve components. Among these are the Basle arrangements for the use of sterling area countries' sterling reserves. The principle is also embodied in the SDR scheme.

It would however be preferable on many counts to convert such voluntary agreements as now exist into international rules for the harmonisation or control of the distribution of reserve component items.

One such scheme for establishing a Reserve Settlement Account with the IMF was outlined in chapter IV, on the Future Role of International Reserve Assets. It can be argued that though it has merits the proposal that each country put its reserve assets on earmark with the IMF might strain the feelings of sovereignty of member countries and was at present impracticable. Similar, earlier proposals have been made and should be considered as part of the readjustment of the international monetary system that must accompany the activation of SDR's.

The problem of the developing countries

The position of the developing countries in relation to the international monetary system is found to be unsatisfactory on account of its insufficient social orientation. It was pointed out that 75 per cent of the newly created SDR's would be allocated to the advanced countries. This would be mitigated if it led to an increase in development finance by the industrial countries.

It is suggested that the industrial countries should earmark a certain proportion of their newly created SDR's for internationally agreed schemes of development or commodity price stabilisation, that would benefit the developing countries. This is one of a number of projects including the Horowitz Plan, which could be considered as a means of constructive assistance to the developing countries. The linkage of additional liquidity-creation and development finance might also have inflationary consequences, especially under conditions of full-employment on account of the transfer of real resources involved. The amount of additional liquidity created should not necessarily be in consonance with development requirements but that liquidity should be created in non-inflationary amounts according to reserve needs.

There is general agreement that the LDC's needed more reserves for a variety of reasons. It is also felt, that there should be structural changes in the working of the international financial institutions to reflect more adequately the LDC's viewpoint. Some feel that one of such improvements could possibly be a more regionally orientated Fund and greater collaboration between Fund and Bank and regional and worldwide organisations, directly concerned with the problems of developing countries.

The more man-managed the monetary system is, the greater would be the need for setting up objective criteria, which should guide the decision-making processes. The possible criteria mentioned are: income per head, potential for growth and the countries' economic performance, the amplitude of balance of payments fluctuations, and relative access to credit facilities.

The socialist countries and the IMF

Though highly desirable, the integration of the Socialist countries into a world-wide monetary system does not seem realisable in the near future. The general feeling of the group entrusted with this topic was that there are still a number of difficulties which have to be overcome before monetary integration is feasible.

The main problems in this regard concern the lack of consistency of pricing structures between Eastern countries and the as yet inadequate development of multilateral trade and payments mechanisms.

The discussions were therefore concentrated on specific ways of assisting the process, within the present framework.

a. an increase in the volume of East-West trade is the first and most important objective.

b. several methods of credit-granting by the West to Eastern countries in order to enable them to adapt more smoothly to the requirements of an international competitive market and to modify their industrial structure accordingly were discussed.

c. it would appear that in certain cases the consolidation of short term debts might assist progress towards convertibility of Eastern currencies.

d. A positive attitude on the part of the Western countries as regards the provision of short and long term finance would be helpful in expanding commercial and financial relationships between East and West.

Postscript

The preceding chapters on the future of the international monetary system were completed on the eve of what was to prove yet another period of serious disturbance in world monetary relations culminating in the devaluation of the French franc and the upvaluation of the mark. This sequence of events emphasizes the main lessons which emerge from them: the need for the closest continuing financial collaboration between the major countries; the essential role in any monetary system of an effective adjustment mechanism to be operated both by deficit and by surplus countries; the special responsibility laid on countries whose currencies are widely used in international trade to maintain reasonable balance in their external payments; the desirability of a somewhat greater measure of flexibility in exchange rates in order to aid this adjustment process; the urgency of the case for supplementing international reserves by a new system of reserve creation in which the supply of additional international liquidity might be determined by the needs of trade and not, as tends to happen now, by the accidents of production and hoarding of gold and by changes in the balances of payments of the reserve currency countries.

On most of these issues there are inevitable differences of opinion as to the manner in which these objectives were to be realised. Such differences are particularly apparent in discussions of the degree to which exchange flexibility should be part of the adjustment process, on the relative weights of responsibility to be placed on deficit and surplus countries for restoring disturbed payments equilibrium, and finally on the role to be played by gold in the future international monetary system.

There is virtual unanimity in the view that no international monetary system can function efficiently without a reasonable measure of discipline which individual countries must apply to their own economic policies. The disturbances which have punctuated the recent course of international monetary affairs, have been caused more by the shortcomings of such discipline than to defects inherent in the system itself.

INDEX OF SUBJECTS AND AUTHORS' NAMES*

Abbreviations used: 15   Note = Footnote

---

* Prepared by J. Douma

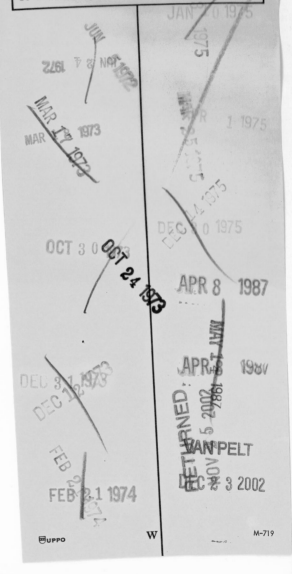